The Gnostic Gospels of Thomas, Mary, and John

The Gnostic Gospels of Thomas, Mary, and John

Gospel of Thomas

The Gospel of Thomas is a collection of traditional Sayings (logoi) of Jesus. It is attributed to Didymos Judas Thomas, the "Doubting Thomas" of the canonical Gospels, and according to many early traditions, the twin brother of Jesus ("didymos" means "twin" in Greek).

We have two versions of the Gospel of Thomas today. The first was discovered in the late 1800's among the Oxyrhynchus Papyri, and consists of fragments of a Greek version, which has been dated to c. 200. The second is a complete version, in Coptic, from Codex II of the Nag Hammadi finds. Thomas was probably first written in Greek (or possibly even Syriac or Aramaic) sometime between the mid 1st and 2nd centuries.

There has been much speculation on the relationship of Thomas to the canonical Gospels. Many Sayings in Thomas have parallels with the New Testament Sayings, especially those found in the synoptic Gospels. This leads many to believe that Thomas was also based on the so-called "Q" Document, along with Matthew, Luke, and Mark. Indeed, some have speculated that Thomas may in fact be "Q". Unlike the synoptic Gospels, and like "Q", the Gospel of Thomas has no narrative connecting the various Sayings. In form, it is simply a list of 114 Sayings, in no particular order. Comparison with New Testament parallels show that Thomas contains either more primitive versions of the Sayings, or developments of more primitive versions. Either way, Thomas seems to preserve earlier traditions about Jesus than the New Testament.

Although it is not possible to attribute the Gospel of Thomas to any particular sect, it is clearly Gnostic in nature. As the preamble indicates, these are "secret sayings", and are intended to be esoteric in nature. The Sayings are not intended to be interpreted literally, as their New Testament parallels often are, but to be interpreted symbolically, as attested by Saying #1. While a literal interpretation may make sense, only by understanding the deeper meanings of the Sayings can one truly understand them. Thus in Saying #114, it is to be understood that "male" symbolizes the pneumatic (spiritual, or Gnostic) Christians, and "female" symbolizes the psychic (unenlightened, or orthodox) Christians, rather than actually referring to males and females. Keep in mind that true understanding of this text was meant to come from PERSONAL contact with the Divine, inspiration from within.

I will now present translations of both the Greek and Coptic versions of the Gospel of Thomas. Of the 114 Sayings in the complete work, and all of the fragments of the Greek text. Also, the Greek version contains one Saying not found in the Coptic version, which comes between Sayings 32 and 33 of the Coptic version. I will enter the Coptic version first, as it is more complete, followed by the Greek version. After both translations, I've provided a listing of New Testament parallels for all 114 sayings for easier comparison.

Note that for the Coptic version, I use the standard NHL translation, except for saying 70, where I have substituted the translation found in Elaine Pagels' "The Gnostic Gospels", as it seems a better translation.

Peace & Enlightenment be yours!

II: Coptic Gospel of Thomas

P)   These are the secret sayings which the living Jesus spoke and which Didymos Judas Thomas wrote down.

1)   And He said, "Whoever finds the interpretation of these sayings will not experience death."

2)   Jesus said, "Let him who seeks continue seeking until he finds. When he finds, he will become troubled. When he becomes troubled, he will be astonished, and he will rule over the All."

3)   Jesus said, "If those who lead you say, 'See, the Kingdom is in the sky,' then the birds of the sky will precede you. If they say to you, 'It is in the sea,' then the fish will precede you. Rather, the Kingdom is inside of you, and it is outside of you. When you come to know yourselves, then you will become known, and you will realize that it is you who are the sons of the living Father. But if you will not know yourselves, you dwell in poverty and it is you who are that poverty."

4)   Jesus said, "The man old in days will not hesitate to ask a small child seven days old about the place of life, and he will live. For many who are first will become last, and they will become one and the same."

5)   Jesus said, "Recognize what is in your sight, and that which is hidden from you will become plain to you. For there is nothing hidden which will not become manifest."

6)   His disciples questioned Him and said to Him, "Do you want us to fast? How shall we pray? Shall we give alms? What diet shall we observe?"

Jesus said, "Do not tell lies, and do not do what you hate, for all things are plain in the sight of Heaven. For nothing hidden will not become manifest, and nothing covered will remain without being uncovered."

7) Jesus said, "Blessed is the lion which becomes man when consumed by man; and cursed is the man whom the lion consumes, and the lion becomes man."

8) And He said, "The Kingdom is like a wise fisherman who cast his net into the sea and drew it up from the sea full of small fish. Among them the wise fisherman found a fine large fish. He threw all the small fish back into the sea and chose the large fish without difficulty. Whoever has ears to hear, let him hear."

9) Jesus said, "Now the sower went out, took a handful (of seeds), and scattered them. Some fell on the road; the birds came and gathered them up. Others fell on the rock, did not take root in the soil, and did not produce ears. And others fell on thorns; they choked the seed(s) and worms ate them. And others fell on the good soil and produced good fruit: it bore sixty per measure and a hundred and twenty per measure."

10) Jesus said, "I have cast fire upon the world, and see, I am guarding it until it blazes."

11) Jesus said, "This heaven will pass away, and the one above it will pass away. The dead are not alive, and the living will not die. In the days when you consumed what is dead, you made it what is alive. When you come to dwell in the light, what will you do? On the day when you were one you became two. But when you become two, what will you do?"

12) The disciples said to Jesus, "We know that You will depart from us. Who is to be our leader?"

Jesus said to them, "Wherever you are, you are to go to James the righteous, for whose sake heaven and earth came into being."

13) Jesus said to His disciples, "Compare me to someone and tell Me whom I am like."

Simon Peter said to Him, "You are like a righteous angel."

Matthew said to Him, "You are like a wise philosopher."

Thomas said to Him, "Master, my mouth is wholly incapable of saying whom You are like."

Jesus said, "I am not your master. Because you have drunk, you have become intoxicated by the bubbling spring which I have measured out."

And He took him and withdrew and told him three things. When Thomas returned to his companions, they asked him, "What did Jesus say to you?"

Thomas said to them, "If I tell you one of the things which he told me, you will pick up stones and throw them at me; a fire will come out of the stones and burn you up."

14) Jesus said to them, "If you fast, you will give rise to sin for yourselves; and if you pray, you will be condemned; and if you give alms, you will do harm to your spirits. When you go into any land and walk about in the districts, if they receive you, eat what they will set before you, and heal the sick among them. For what goes into your mouth will not defile you, but that which issues from your mouth - it is that which will defile you."

15) Jesus said, "When you see one who was not born of woman, prostrate yourselves on your faces and worship him. That one is your Father."

16) Jesus said, "Men think, perhaps, that it is peace which I have come to cast upon the world. They do not know that it is dissension which I have come to cast upon the earth: fire, sword, and war. For there will be five in a house: three will be against two, and two against three, the father against the son, and the son against the father. And they will stand solitary."

17) Jesus said, "I shall give you what no eye has seen and what no ear has heard and what no hand has touched and what has never occurred to the human mind."

18) The disciples said to Jesus, "Tell us how our end will be."

Jesus said, "Have you discovered, then, the beginning, that you look for the end? For where the beginning is, there will the end be.

Blessed is he who will take his place in the beginning; he will know the end and will not experience death."

19) Jesus said, "Blessed is he who came into being before he came into being. If you become My disciples and listen to My words, these stones will minister to you. For there are five trees for you in Paradise which remain undisturbed summer and winter and whose leaves do not fall. Whoever becomes acquainted with them will not experience death."

20) The disciples said to Jesus, "Tell us what the Kingdom of Heaven is like."

He said to them, "It is like a mustard seed, the smallest of all seeds. But when it falls on tilled soil, it produces a great plant and becomes a shelter for birds of the sky."

21) Mary said to Jesus, "Whom are Your disciples like?"

He said, "They are like children who have settled in a field which is not theirs. When the owners of the field come, they will say, 'Let us have back our field.' They (will) undress in their presence in order to let them have back their field and give it back to them. Therefore I say to you, if the owner of a house knows that the thief is coming, he will begin his vigil before he comes and will not let him into his house of his domain to carry away his goods. You, then, be on your guard against the world. Arm yourselves with great strength lest the robbers find a way to come to you, for the difficulty which you expect will (surely) materialize. Let there be among you a man of understanding. When the grain ripened, he came quickly with his sickle in his hand and reaped it. Whoever has ears to hear, let him hear."

22) Jesus saw infants being suckled. He said to His disciples, "These infants being suckled are like those who enter the Kingdom."

They said to Him, "Shall we then, as children, enter the Kingdom?"

Jesus said to them, "When you make the two one, and when you make the inside like the outside and the outside like the inside, and the above like the below, and when you make the male and the female one and the same, so that the male not be male nor the female female; and when you fashion eyes in the place of an eye, and a hand in place of a hand, and a foot in place of a foot, and a likeness in place of a likeness; then will you enter [the Kingdom]."

23) Jesus said, "I shall choose you, one out of a thousand, and two out of ten thousand, and they shall stand as a single one."

24) His disciples said to Him, "Show us the place where You are, since it is necessary for us to seek it."

He said to them, "Whoever has ears, let him hear. There is light within a man of light, and he (or "it") lights up the whole world. If he (or "it") does not shine, he (or "it") is darkness."

25) Jesus said, "Love your brother like your soul, guard him like the pupil of your eye."

26) Jesus said, "You see the mote in your brothers eye, but you do not see the beam in your own eye. When you cast the beam out of your own eye, then you will see clearly to cast the mote from your brother's eye."

27) Jesus said, "If you do not fast as regards the world, you will not find the Kingdom. If you do not observe the Sabbath as a Sabbath, you will not see the Father."

28) Jesus said, "I took my place in the midst of the world, and I appeared to them in the flesh. I found all of them intoxicated; I found none of them thirsty. And My soul became afflicted for the sons of men, because they are blind in their hearts and do not have sight; for empty they came into the world, and empty too they seek to leave the world. But for the moment they are intoxicated. When they shake off their wine, then they will repent."

29) Jesus said, "If the flesh came into being because of spirit, it is a wonder. But if spirit came into being because of the body, it is a wonder of wonders. Indeed, I am amazed at how this great wealth has made its home in this poverty."

30) Jesus said, "Where there are three gods, they are gods. Where there are two or one, I am with him."

31) Jesus said, "No prophet is accepted in his own village; no physician heals those who know him." 32) Jesus said, "A city being built on a high mountain and fortified cannot fall, nor can it be hidden."

33) Jesus said, "Preach from your housetops that which you will hear in your ear {(and) in the other ear}. For no one lights a lamp and puts it under a bushel, nor does he put it in a hidden place, but rather he sets it on a lampstand so that everyone who enters and leaves will see its light."

34) Jesus said, "If a blind man leads a blind man, they will both fall into a pit."

35) Jesus said, "It is not possible for anyone to enter the house of a strong man and take it by force unless he binds his hands; then he will (be able to) ransack his house."

36) Jesus said, "Do not be concerned from morning until evening and from evening until morning about what you will wear."

37) His disciples said, "When will You become revealed to us and when shall we see You?"

Jesus said, "When you disrobe without being ashamed and take up your garments and place them under your feet like little children and tread on them, then [will you see] the Son of the Living One, and you will not be afraid"

38) Jesus said, "Many times have you desired to hear these words which I am saying to you, and you have no one else to hear them from. There will be days when you look for Me and will not find Me."

39) Jesus said, "The Pharisees and the scribes have taken the keys of Knowledge and hidden them. They themselves have not entered, nor have they allowed to enter those who wish to. You, however, be as wise as serpents and as innocent as doves."

40) Jesus said, "A grapevine has been planted outside of the Father, but being unsound, it will be pulled up by its roots and destroyed."

41) Jesus said, "Whoever has something in his hand will receive

more, and whoever has nothing will be deprived of even the little he has."

42) Jesus said, "Become passers-by."

43) His disciples said to him, "Who are You, that You should say these things to us?"

Jesus said to them, "You do not realize who I am from what I say to you, but you have become like the Jews, for they (either) love the tree and hate its fruit or love the fruit and hate the tree."

44) Jesus said, "Whoever blasphemes against the Father will be forgiven, and whoever blasphemes against the Son will be forgiven, but whoever blasphemes against the Holy Spirit will not be forgiven either on earth or in heaven."

45) Jesus said, "Grapes are not harvested from thorns, nor are figs gathered from thistles, for they do not produce fruit. A good man brings forth good from his storehouse; an evil man brings forth evil things from his evil storehouse, which is in his heart, and says evil things. For out of the abundance of the heart he brings forth evil things."

46) Jesus said, "Among those born of women, from Adam until John the Baptist, there is no one so superior to John the Baptist that his eyes should not be lowered (before him). Yet I have said whichever one of you comes to be a child will be acquainted with the Kingdom and will become superior to John."

47) Jesus said, "It is impossible for a man to mount two horses or to stretch two bows. And it is impossible for a servant to serve two masters; otherwise he will honor the one and treat the other contemptuously. No man drinks old wine and immediately desires to drink new wine. And new wine is not put into old wineskins, lest they burst; nor is old wine put into a new wineskin, lest it spoil it. An old patch is not sewn onto a new garment, because a tear would result."

48) Jesus said, "If two make peace with each other in this one house, they will say to the mountain, 'Move Away,' and it will move away."

49) Jesus said, "Blessed are the solitary and elect, for you will find the Kingdom. For you are from it, and to it you will return."

50) Jesus said, "If they say to you, 'Where did you come from?', say to them, 'We came from the light, the place where the light came into being on its own accord and established [itself] and became manifest through their image.' If they say to you, 'Is it you?', say, 'We are its children, we are the elect of the Living Father.' If they ask you, 'What is the sign of your father in you?', say to them, 'It is movement and repose.'"

51) His disciples said to Him, "When will the repose of the dead come about, and when will the new world come?"

He said to them, "What you look forward to has already come, but you do not recognize it."

52) His disciples said to Him, "Twenty-four prophets spoke in Israel, and all of them spoke in You."

He said to them, "You have omitted the one living in your presence and have spoken (only) of the dead."

53) His disciples said to Him, "Is circumcision beneficial or not?"

He said to them, "If it were beneficial, their father would beget them already circumcised from their mother. Rather, the true circumcision in spirit has become completely profitable."

54) Jesus said, "Blessed are the poor, for yours is the Kingdom of Heaven."

55) Jesus said, "Whoever does not hate his father and his mother cannot become a disciple to Me. And whoever does not hate his brothers and sisters and take up his cross in My way will not be worthy of Me."

56) Jesus said, "Whoever has come to understand the world has found (only) a corpse, and whoever has found a corpse is superior to the world."

57) Jesus said, "The Kingdom of the Father is like a man who had [good] seed. His enemy came by night and sowed weeds among the good seed. The man did not allow them to pull up the weeds; he said

to them, 'I am afraid that you will go intending to pull up the weeds and pull up the wheat along with them.' For on the day of the harvest the weeds will be plainly visible, and they will be pulled up and burned."

58) Jesus said, "Blessed is the man who has suffered and found life."

59) Jesus said, "Take heed of the Living One while you are alive, lest you die and seek to see Him and be unable to do so."

60) They saw a Samaritan carrying a lamb on his way to Judea. He said to his disciples, "(Why does) that man (carry) the lamb around?"

They said to him, "So that he may kill it and eat it."

He said to them, "While it is alive, he will not eat it, but only when he has killed it and it has become a corpse."

They said to him, "He cannot do so otherwise."

He said to them, "You too, look for a place for yourself within the Repose, lest you become a corpse and be eaten."

61) Jesus said, "Two will rest on a bed: the one will die, and other will live."

Salome said to him, "Who are You, man, that You, as though from the One, have come up on my couch and eaten from my table?"

Jesus said to her, "I am He who exists from the Undivided. I was given some of the things of my Father."

Salome said, "I am Your disciple."

Jesus said to her, "Therefore I say, if he is undivided, he will be filled with light, but if he is divided, he will be filled with darkness."

62) Jesus said, "It is to those [who are worthy of My] mysteries that I tell My mysteries. Do not let your left hand know what your right hand is doing." 63) Jesus said, "There was a rich man who had much money. He said, 'I shall put my money to use so that I may sow, reap, plant, and fill my storehouse with produce, with the result that I shall lack nothing. Such were his intentions, but that same night he died. Let him who has ears hear."

64) Jesus said, "A man had received visitors. And when he had

prepared the dinner, he sent his servant to invite guests. He went to the first one and said to him, "My master invites you.' He said, 'I have claims against some merchants. They are coming to me this evening. I must go and give them my orders. I ask to be excused from the dinner.' He went to another and said, 'My master has invited you.' He said to him, 'I have just bought a house and am required for the day. I shall not have any spare time.' He went to another and said to him, 'My master invites you.' He said to him, 'My friend is going to get married, and I am to prepare the banquet. I shall not be able to come. I ask to be excused from the dinner.' He went to another and said to him, 'My master invites you.' He said to him, 'I have just bought a farm, and I am on my way to collect the rent. I shall not be able to come. I ask to be excused.' The servant returned and said to his master, 'Those whom you invited to the dinner have asked to be excused.' The master said to his servant, 'Go outside to the streets and bring back those whom you happen to meet, so that they may dine.' Businessmen and merchants will not enter the Places of My Father."

65) He said, "There was a good man who owned a vineyard. He leased it to tenant farmers so that they might work it and he might collect the produce from them. He sent his servant so that the tenants might give him the produce of the vineyard. They seized his servant and beat him, all but killing him. The servant went back and told his master. The master said, 'Perhaps they did not recognize him.' He sent another servant. The tenants beat this one as well. Then the owner sent his son and said, 'Perhaps they will show respect to my son.' Because the tenants knew that it was he who was the heir to the vineyard, they seized him and killed him. Let him who has ears hear."

66) Jesus said, "Show me the stone which the builders have rejected. That one is the cornerstone."

67) Jesus said, "Whoever believes that the All itself is deficient is (himself) completely deficient."

68) Jesus said, "Blessed are you when you are hated and

persecuted. Wherever you have been persecuted they will find no Place."

69) Jesus said, "Blessed are they who have been persecuted within themselves. It is they who have truly come to know the Father. Blessed are the hungry, for the belly of him who desires will be filled."

70) Jesus said, "If you bring forth what is within you, what you bring forth will save you. If you do not bring forth what is within you, what you do not bring forth will destroy you."

71) Jesus said, "I shall destroy [this] house, and no one will be able to rebuild it."

72) [A man said] to Him, "Tell my brothers to divide my father's possessions with me."

He said to him, "O man, who has made Me a divider?"

He turned to His disciples and said to them, "I am not a divider, am I?"

73) Jesus said, "The harvest is great but the laborers are few. Beseech the Lord, therefore, to send out laborers to the harvest."

74) He said, "O Lord, there are many around the drinking trough, but there is nothing in the cistern."

75) Jesus said, "Many are standing at the door, but it is the solitary who will enter the bridal chamber."

76) Jesus said, "The kingdom of the Father is like a merchant who had a consignment of merchandise and who discovered a pearl. That merchant was shrewd. He sold the merchandise and bought the pearl alone for himself. You too, seek his unfailing and enduring treasure where no moth comes near to devour and no worm destroys."

77) Jesus said, "It is I who am the light which is above them all. It is I who am the All. From Me did the All come forth, and unto Me did the All extend. Split a piece of wood, and I am there. Lift up the stone, and you will find Me there."

78) Jesus said, "Why have you come out into the desert? To see a reed shaken by the wind? And to see a man clothed in fine garments like your kings and your great men? Upon them are the fine

[garments], and they are unable to discern the truth."

79) A woman from the crowd said to Him, "Blessed are the womb which bore You and the breasts which nourished You."

He said to her, "Blessed are those who have heard the word of the Father and have truly kept it. For there will be days when you will say, 'Blessed are the womb which has not conceived and the breasts which have not given milk.'"

80) Jesus said, "He who has recognized the world has found the body, but he who has found the body is superior to the world."

81) Jesus said, "Let him who has grown rich be king, and let him who possesses power renounce it."

82) Jesus said, "He who is near Me is near the fire, and he who is far from Me is far from the Kingdom."

83) Jesus said, "The images are manifest to man, but the light in them remains concealed in the image of the light of the Father. He will become manifest, but his image will remain concealed by his light."

84) Jesus said, "When you see your likeness, you rejoice. But when you see your images which came into being before you, and which neither die not become manifest, how much you will have to bear!"

85) Jesus said, "Adam came into being from a great power and a great wealth, but he did not become worthy of you. For had he been worthy, [he would] not [have experienced] death."

86) Jesus said, "[The foxes have their holes] and the birds have [their] nests, but the Son of Man has no place to lay his head and rest."

87) Jesus said, "Wretched is the body that is dependant upon a body, and wretched is the soul that is dependent on these two."

88) Jesus said, "The angels and the prophets will come to you and give you those things you (already) have. And you too, give them those things which you have, and say to yourselves, 'When will they come and take what is theirs?'"

89) Jesus said, "Why do you wash the outside of the cup? Do you not realize that he who made he inside is the same one who made the outside?"

90) Jesus said, "Come unto me, for My yoke is easy and My lordship is mild, and you will find repose for yourselves."

91) They said to Him, "Tell us who You are so that we may believe in You."

He said to them, "You read the face of the sky and of the earth, but you have not recognized the one who is before you, and you do not know how to read this moment."

92) Jesus said, "Seek and you will find. Yet, what you asked Me about in former times and which I did not tell you then, now I do desire to tell, but you do not enquire after it."

93) Jesus said, "Do not give what is holy to dogs, lest they throw them on the dung-heap. Do not throw the pearls to swine, lest they grind it [to bits]."

94) Jesus [said], "He who seeks will find, and [he who knocks] will be let in."

95) [Jesus said,] "If you have money, do not lend it at interest, but give [it] to one from whom you will not get it back."

96) Jesus [said], "The Kingdom of the Father is like a certain woman. She took a little leaven, [concealed] it in some dough, and made it into large loaves. Let him who has ears hear."

97) Jesus said, "The Kingdom of the [Father] is like a certain woman who was carrying a jar full of meal. While she was walking [on] a road, still some distance from home, the handle of the jar broke and the meal emptied out behind her on the road. She did not realize it; she had noticed no accident. When she reached her house, she set the jar down and found it empty."

98) Jesus said, "The Kingdom of the Father is like a certain man who wanted to kill a powerful man. In his own house he drew his sword and stuck it into the wall in order to find out whether his hand could carry through. Then he slew the powerful man."

99) The disciples said to Him, "Your brothers and Your mother are standing outside."

He said to them, "Those here who do the will of My Father are My brothers and My mother. It is they who will enter the Kingdom of My Father."

100) They showed Jesus a gold coin and said to Him, "Caesar's men demand taxes from us."

He said to them, "Give Caesar what belongs to Caesar, give God what belongs to God, and give Me what is Mine."

101) Jesus said, "Whoever does not hate his father and his mother as I do cannot become a disciple to Me. And whoever does [not] love his father and his mother as I do cannot become a [disciple] to Me. For My mother [gave me falsehood], but [My] true [Mother] gave me life."

102) Jesus said, "Woe to the Pharisees, for they are like a dog sleeping in the manger of oxen, for neither does he eat nor does he let the oxen eat."

103) Jesus said, "Fortunate is the man who knows where the brigands will enter, so that he may get up, muster his domain, and arm himself before they invade."

104) They said [to Jesus], "Come, let us pray today and let us fast."

Jesus said, "What is the sin that I have committed, or wherein have I been defeated? But when the bridegroom leaves the bridal chamber, then let them fast and pray."

105) Jesus said, "He who knows the father and the mother will be called the son of a harlot."

106) Jesus said, "When you make the two one, you will become the sons of man, and when you say, 'Mountain, move away,' it will move away."

107) Jesus said, "The Kingdom is like a shepherd who had a hundred sheep. One of them, the largest, went astray. He left the ninety-nine sheep and looked for that one until he found it. When he had gone to such trouble, he said to the sheep, 'I care for you more

than the ninety-nine.'"

108) Jesus said, "He who will drink from my mouth will become like Me. I myself shall become he, and the things that are hidden will become revealed to him."

109) Jesus said, "The Kingdom is like a man who had a [hidden] treasure in his field without knowing it. And [after] he died, he left it to his son. The son did not know (about the treasure). He inherited the field and sold [it]. And the one who bought it went plowing and found the treasure. He began to lend money at interest to whomever he wished."

110) Jesus said, "Whoever finds the world and becomes rich, let him renounce the world."

111) Jesus said, "The heavens and the earth will be rolled up in your presence. And one who lives from the Living One will not see death." Does not Jesus say, "Whoever finds himself is superior to the world?"

112) Jesus said, "Woe to the flesh that depends on the soul; woe to the soul that depends on the flesh."

113) His disciples said to Him, "When will the Kingdom come?"

Jesus said, "It will not come by waiting for it. It will not be a matter of saying 'Here it is' or 'There it is.' Rather, the Kingdom of the Father is spread out upon the earth, and men do not see it."

114) Simon Peter said to Him, "Let Mary leave us, for women are not worthy of Life."

Jesus said, "I myself shall lead her in order to make her male, so that she too may become a living spirit resembling you males. For every woman who will make herself male will enter the Kingdom of Heaven."

III: Fragments of Greek Gospel of Thomas

Several fragments of a Greek version of Thomas were found among the Oxyrhynchys Papyri in the late 19th century. These fragments consist of the preamble, and sayings 1-6, 26-28, 30-32, 36-38, and 39, as well as a saying not found in the Coptic version, which follows 32. These fragments are found on Oxyrhynchus Papyri 1, 654, and 655. Generally, the sayings are essentially the same in both versions. However, the equivalent of saying 30 adds the end of the Coptic version's saying 77.

The translation used here is a combination of thranslations by B.P. Grenfell and A.S. Hunt and Bentley Layton.

P)   These are the secret sayings which were spoken by Jesus the Living One, and which Judas, who is called Thomas, wrote down"

1) He said to them: "Whoever hears these words shall never taste death."

2) [Jesus said]: "Let him who seeks not cease until he finds, and when he finds he shall wonder; wondering he shall reign, and reigning shall rest."

3) Jesus said, "If those who attract you say, 'See, the Kingdom is in the sky,' then the birds of the sky will precede you. If they say to you, 'It is under the earth,' then the fish of the sea will precede you. Rather, the Kingdom of God is inside of you, and it is outside of you. [Those who] become acquainted with [themselves] will find it; [and when you] become acquainted with yourselves, [you will understand that] it is you who are the sons of the living Father. But if you will not

know yourselves, you dwell in poverty and it is you who are that poverty."

4) Jesus said: "Let the old man who is full of days not hesitate to ask the child of seven days about the place of life; then he will live. For many that are first will be last, and last, first, and they will become a single one."

5) Jesus said: "Recognize what is before your face and that which is hidden from the you will be revealed to you. For there is nothing hidden which shall not be made manifest, nor buried which shall not be raised."

6) His disciples asked him and said to him, "How do you want us to fast? And how shall we pray? And how [shall we] give alms? And what kind of diet shall we follow?"

Jesus said, "Do not lie, and do not do what you hate, for all things are disclosed before truth. For there is nothing hidden which shall not be shown forth."

27) Jesus said: "Unless you fast to the world, you shall in no way find the Kingdom of God; and unless you sabbatize the Sabbath, you shall not see the Father."

28) Jesus said: "I stood in the midst of the world, and in the flesh I was seen by them, and I found all drunken, and I found none among them thirsty. And my soul grieved over the souls of men, because they are blind in their heart and see not. [...]

30/77) Jesus said: "Where there are [two, they are not] without God, and when there is one alone, [I say,] I am with him. Raise the stone, and there you will find me; cleave the wood, and there I am."

31) Jesus said: "A prophet is not acceptable in his own country, neither does a physician work cures upon those that know him."

32) Jesus said: "A city built on the top of a high hill and fortified can neither fall nor be hid."

—) Jesus said: "Thou hearest with one ear, [but the other thou has closed].

36) Jesus said, "Do not worry from dawn to dusk and from dusk to

dawn about [what food] you [will] eat, [or] what [clothing] you will wear. [You are much] better than the [lilies], which [neither] card nor spin. And for your part, what [will you wear] when you have no clothing? Who would add to your stature? It is he who will give you your clothing.

37) His disciples said to him, "When will you be visible to us, and when shall we behold you?"

He said, "When you strip naked without being ashamed, and take your garments and put them under your feet like little children and tread upon them, then you will see the child of the Living, and you will not be afraid."

IV: Canonical Comparisons of Thomas Sayings

I have grouped the sayings in the Gospel of Thomas into 5 categories. Sayings that are variants of or close parallels to canonical passages (22 of these), sayings that appear more remotely parallel or similar in some way (28), sayings which contain parts parallel to several unconnected passages (13), sayings parallel to non-canonical traditions of Jesus (only 1 of these), and those with no apparent parallels (50!).

Due to space limitations, I have decided only to cite passages, and you can go through and compare them using any Bible. I haven't attempted to make any comparisons to the various Apocryphal or other Christian and Gnostic texts.

Excerpts from the Gospel of Mary

[The Coptic papyrus, from which the first six pages have been lost, begins in the middle of this gospel.]

"...will, then, matter be saved or not?"

The Savior said, "All natures, all formed things, all creatures exist in and with one another and will again be resolved into their own roots, because the nature of matter is dissolved into the roots of its nature alone. He who has ears to hear, let him hear." [cf. Matt. 11:15, etc.].

Peter said to him, "Since you have now explained all things to us, tell us this: what is the sin of the world?" [cf. John 1:29]. The Savior said, "Sin as such does not exist, but you make sin when you do what is of the nature of fornication, which is called 'sin.' For this reason the Good came into your midst, to the essence of each nature, to restore it to its root." He went on to say, "For this reason you come into existence and die [...] whoever knows may know [...] a suffering which has nothing like itself, which has arisen out of what is contrary to nature. Then there arises a disturbance in the whole body. For this reason I said to you, Be of good courage [cf. Matt. 28:9], and if you are discouraged, still take courage over against the various forms of nature. He who has ears to hear, let him hear." When the Blessed One said this, he greeted all of them, saying "Peace be with you [cf. John 14:27]. Receive my peace for yourselves. Take heed lest anyone lead you astray with the words, 'Lo, here!' or 'Lo, there!' [cf. Matt. 24:5, 23; Luke 17:21] for the Son of Man is within you [cf. Luke 17:21]. Follow him; those who seek him will find him [cf. Matt. 7:7]. Go, therefore, and preach the Gospel of the Kingdom [cf. Matt. 4:23;

9:15; Mark 16:15]. I have left no commandment but what I have commanded you, and I have given you no law, as the lawgiver did, lest you be bound by it."

They grieved and mourned greatly, saying, "How shall we go to the Gentiles and preach the Gospel of the Kingdom of the Son of Man? If even he was not spared, how shall we be spared?"

Then Mary stood up and greeted all of them and said to her brethren, "Do not mourn or grieve or be irresolute, for his grace will be with you all and will defend you. Let us rather praise his greatness, for he prepared us and made us into men." When Mary said this, their hearts changed for the better, and they began to discuss the words of the [Savior].

Peter said to Mary, "Sister, we know that the Savior loved you more than other women [cf. John 11:5, Luke 10:38-42]. Tell us the words of the Savior which you have in mind since you know them; and we do not, nor have we heard of them."

Mary answered and said, "What is hidden from you I will impart to you." And she began to say the following words to them. "I," she said, "I saw the Lord in a vision and I said to him, 'Lord, I saw you today in a vision.' He answered and said to me, 'Blessed are you, since you did not waver at the sight of me. For where the mind is, there is your countenance' [cf. Matt. 6:21]. I said to him, 'Lord, the mind which sees the vision, does it see it through the soul or through the spirit?' The Savior answered and said, 'It sees neither through the soul nor through the spirit, but the mind, which is between the two, which sees the vision, and it is...'"

"...and Desire said, 'I did not see you descend; but now I see you rising. Why do you speak falsely, when you belong to me?' The soul answered and said, 'I saw you, but you did not see me or recognize me; I served you as a garment and you did not recognize me.' After it had said this, it went joyfully and gladly away. Again it came to the third power, Ignorance. This power questioned the soul: 'Whither are you going? You were bound in wickedness, you were bound indeed.

Judge not' [cf. Matt. 7:1]. And the soul said, 'Why do you judge me, when I judged not? I was bound, though I did not bind. I was not recognized, but I recognized that all will go free, things both earthly and heavenly.' After the soul had left the third power behind, it rose upward, and saw the fourth power, which had seven forms. The first form is darkness, the second desire, the third ignorance, the fourth the arousing of death, the fifth is the kingdom of the flesh, the sixth is the wisdom of the folly of the flesh, the seventh is wrathful wisdom. These are the seven participants in wrath. They ask the soul, 'Whence do you come, killer of men, or where are you going, conqueror of space?' The soul answered and said, 'What seizes me is killed; what turns me about is overcome; my desire has come to an end and ignorance is dead. In a world I was saved from a world, and in a "type," from a higher "type" and from the fetter of the impotence of knowledge, the existence of which is temporal. From this time I will reach rest in the time of the moment of the Aeon in silence.'"

When Mary had said this, she was silent, since the Savior had spoken thus far with her. But Andrew answered and said to the brethren, 'Say what you think concerning what she said. For I do not believe that the Savior said this. For certainly these teachings are of other ideas."

Peter also opposed her in regard to these matters and asked them about the Savior. "Did he then speak secretly with a woman [cf. John 4:27], in preference to us, and not openly? Are we to turn back and all listen to her? Did he prefer her to us?" Then Mary grieved and said to Peter, "My brother Peter, what do you think? Do you think that I thought this up myself in my heart or that I am lying concerning the Savior?"

Levi answered and said to Peter, "Peter, you are always irate. Now I see that you are contending against the woman like the adversaries. But if the Savior made her worthy, who are you to reject her? Surely the Savior knew her very well [cf. Luke 10:38- 42]. For this reason he loved her more than us [cf. John 11:5]. And we should rather be ashamed and put on the Perfect Man, to form us [?] as he commanded us, and proclaim the gospel, without publishing a further commandment or a further law than the one which the Savior spoke." When Levi had said this, they began to go out in order to proclaim him and preach him.

The Acts of John

18 Now John was hastening to Ephesus, moved thereto by a vision. Damonicus therefore, and Aristodemus his kinsman, and a certain very rich man Cleobius, and the wife of Marcellus, hardly prevailed to keep him for one day in Miletus, reposing themselves with him. And when very early in the morning they had set forth, and already about four miles of the journey were accomplished, a voice came from heaven in the hearing of all of us, saying: John, thou art about to give glory to thy Lord in Ephesus, whereof thou shalt know, thou and all the brethren that are with thee, and certain of them that are there, which shall believe by thy means. John therefore pondered, rejoicing in himself, what it should be that should befall (meet) him at Ephesus, and said: Lord, behold I go according to thy will: let that be done which thou desirest.

19 And as we drew near to the city, Lycomedes the praetor of the Ephesians, a man of large substance, met us, and falling at John's feet besought him, saying: Is thy name John? the God whom thou preachest hath sent thee to do good unto my wife, who hath been smitten with palsy now these seven days and lieth incurable. But glorify thou thy God by healing her, and have compassion on us. For as I was considering with myself what resolve to take in this matter, one stood by me and said: Lycomedes, cease from this thought which warreth against thee, for it is evil (hard): submit not thyself unto it. For I have compassion upon mine handmaid Cleopatra, and have sent from Miletus a man named John who shall raise her up and restore her to thee whole. Tarry not, therefore, thou servant of the God who hath manifested himself unto me, but hasten unto my wife

who hath no more than breath. And straightway John went from the gate, with the brethren that were with him and Lycomedes, unto his house. But Cleobius said to his young men: Go ye to my kinsman Callippus and receive of him comfortable entertainment -for I am come hither with his son- that we may find all things decent.

20 Now when Lycomedes came with John into the house wherein his wife lay, he caught hold again of his feet and said: See, lord, the withering of the beauty, see the youth, see the renowned flower of my poor wife, whereat all Ephesus was wont to marvel: wretched me, I have suffered envy, I have been humbled, the eye of mine enemies hath smitten me: I have never wronged any, though I might have injured many, for I looked before to this very thing, and took care, lest I should see any evil or any such ill fortune as this. What profit, then, hath Cleopatra from my anxiety? what have I gained by being known for a pious man until this day? nay, I suffer more than the impious, in that I see thee, Cleopatra, lying in such plight. The sun in his course shall no more see me conversing with thee: I will go before thee, Cleopatra, and rid myself of life: I will not spare mine own safety though it be yet young. I will defend myself before Justice, that I have rightly deserted, for I may indict her as judging unrighteously. I will be avenged on her when I come before her as a ghost [bereft] of life. I will say to her: Thou didst force me to leave the light when thou didst rob me of Cleopatra: thou didst cause me to become a corpse when thou sentest me this ill fortune: thou didst compel me to insult Providence, by cutting off my joy in life (my con- fidence).

21 And with yet more words Lycomedes addressing Cleopatra came near to the bed and cried aloud and lamented: but John pulled him away, and said: Cease from these lamentations and from thine unfitting words: thou must not disobey him that (?) appeared unto thee: for know that thou shalt receive thy consort again. Stand, therefore, with us that have come hither on her account and pray to the God whom thou sawest manifesting himself unto thee in dreams. What, then, is it, Lycomedes? Awake, thou also, and open thy soul.

Cast off the heavy sleep from thee: beseech the Lord, entreat him for thy wife, and he will raise her up. But he fell upon the floor and lamented, fainting. [It is evident from what follows that Lycomedes died: but the text does not say so; some words may have fallen out.]

John therefore said with tears: Alas for the fresh (new) betraying of my vision! for the new temptation that is prepared for me! for the new device of him that contriveth against me! the voice from heaven that was borne unto me in the way, hath it devised this for me? was it this that it foreshowed me should come to pass here, betraying me to this great multitude of the citizens because of Lycomedes? the man lieth without breath, and I know well that they will not suffer me to go out of the house alive. Why tarriest thou, Lord (or, what wilt thou do)? why hast thou shut off from us thy good promise? Do not, I beseech thee, Lord, do not give him cause to exult who rejoiceth in the suffering of others; give him not cause to dance who alway derideth us; but let thy holy name and thy mercy make haste. Raise up these two dead whose death is against me.

22 And even as John thus cried out, the city of the Ephesians ran together to the house of Lycomedes, hearing that he was dead. And John, beholding the great multitude that was come, said unto the Lord: Now is the time of refreshment and of confidence toward thee, O Christ; now is the time for us who are sick to have the help that is of thee, O physician who healest freely; keep thou mine entering in hither safe from derision. I beseech thee, Jesu, succour this great multitude that it may come to thee who art Lord of all things: behold the affliction, behold them that lie here. Do thou prepare, even from them that are assembled for that end, holy vessels for thy service, when they behold thy gift. For thyself hast said, O Christ, 'Ask, and it shall be given you'. We ask therefore of thee, O king, not gold, not silver, not substance, not possessions, nor aught of what is on earth and perisheth, but two souls, by whom thou shalt convert them that are here unto thy way, unto thy teaching, unto thy liberty (confidence), unto thy most excellent (or unfailing) promise: for when

they perceive thy power in that those that have died are raised, they will be saved, some of them. Do thou thyself, therefore, give them hope in thee: and so go I unto Cleopatra and say: Arise in the name of Jesus Christ.

23 And he came to her and touched her face and said: Cleopatra, He saith, whom every ruler feareth, and every creature and every power, the abyss and all darkness, and unsmiling death, and the height of heaven, and the circles of hell [and the resurrection of the dead, and the sight of the blind], and the whole power of the prince of this world, and the pride of the ruler: Arise, and be not an occasion unto many that desire not to believe, or an affliction unto souls that are able to hope and to be saved. And Cleopatra straightway cried with a loud voice: I arise, master: save thou thine handmaid.

Now when she had arisen [who for incurable lain had] seven days, the city of the Ephesians was moved at the unlooked -for sight. And Cleopatra asked concerning her husband Lycomedes, but John said to her: Cleopatra, if thou keep thy soul unmoved and steadfast, thou shalt forthwith have Lycomedes thine husband standing here beside thee, if at least thou be not disturbed nor moved at that which hath befallen, having believed on my God, who by my means shall grant him unto thee alive. Come therefore with me into thine other bedchamber, and thou shalt behold him, a dead corpse indeed, but raised again by the power of my God.

24 And Cleopatra going with John into her bedchamber, and seeing Lycomedes dead for her sake, had no power to speak (suffered in her voice), and ground her teeth and bit her tongue, and closed her eyes, raining down tears: and with calmness gave heed to the apostle. But John had compassion on Cleopatra when he saw that she neither raged nor was beside herself, and called upon the perfect and condescending mercy, saying: Lord Jesus Christ, thou seest the pressure of sorrow, thou seest the need; thou seest Cleopatra shrieking her soul out in silence, for she constraineth within her the frenzy that cannot be borne; and I know that for Lycomedes' sake she

also will die upon his body. And she said quietly to John: That have I in mind, master, and nought else.

And the apostle went to the couch whereon Lycomedes lay, and taking Cleopatra's hand he said: Cleopatra, because of the multitude that is present, and thy kinsfolk that have come in, with strong crying, say thou to thine husband: Arise and glorify the name of God, for he giveth back the dead to the dead. And she went to her husband and said to him according as she was taught, and forthwith raised him up. And he, when he arose, fell on the floor and kissed John's feet, but he raised him, saying: O man, kiss not my feet but the feet of God by whose power ye are both arisen.

25 But Lycomedes said to John: I entreat and adjure thee by the God in whose name thou hast raised us, to abide with us, together with all them that are with thee. Likewise Cleopatra also caught his feet and said the same. And John said to them: For tomorrow I will be with you. And they said to him again: We shall have no hope in thy God, but shall have been raised to no purpose, if thou abide not with us. And Cleobius with Aristodemus and Damonicus were touched in the soul and said to John: Let us abide with them, that they continue without offence towards the Lord. So he continued there with the brethren.

26 There came together therefore a gathering of a great multitude on John's account; and as he discoursed to them that were there, Lycomedes, who had a friend who was a skilful painter, went hastily to him and said to him: You see me in a great hurry to come to you: come quickly to my house and paint the man whom I show you without his knowing it. And the painter, giving some one the necessary implements and colours, said to Lycomedes: Show him to me, and for the rest have no anxiety. And Lycomedes pointed out John to the painter, and brought him near him, and shut him up in a room from which the apostle of Christ could be seen. And Lycomedes was with the blessed man, feasting on the faith and the knowledge of our God, and rejoiced yet more in the thought that he should possess

him in a portrait.

27 The painter, then, on the first day made an outline of him and went away. And on the next he painted him in with his colours, and so delivered the portrait to Lycomedes to his great joy. And lie took it and set it up in his own bedehamber and hung it with garlands: so that later John, when he perceived it, said to him: My beloved child, what is it that thou always doest when thou comest in from the bath into thy bedchamber alone? do not I pray with thee and the rest of the brethren? or is there something thou art hiding from us? And as he said this and talked jestingly with him, he went into the bedchamber, and saw the portrait of an old man crowned with garlands, and lamps and altars set before it. And he called him and said: Lycomedes, what meanest thou by this matter of the portrait? can it be one of thy gods that is painted here? for I see that thou art still living in heathen fashion. And Lycomedes answered him: My only God is he who raised me up from death with my wife: but if, next to that God, it be right that the men who have benefited us should be called gods -it is thou, father, whom I have had painted in that portrait, whom I crown and love and reverence as having become my good guide.

28 And John who had never at any time seen his own face said to him: Thou mockest me, child: am I like that in form, [excelling] thy Lord? how canst thou persuade me that the portrait is like me? And Lycomedes brought him a mirror. And when he had seen himself in the mirror and looked earnestly at the portrait, he said: As the Lord Jesus Christ liveth, the portrait is like me: yet not like me, child, but like my fleshly image; for if this painter, who hath imitated this my face, desireth to draw me in a portrait, he will be at a loss, [needing more than] the colours that are now given to thee, and boards and plaster (?) and glue (?), and the position of my shape, and old age and youth and all things that are seen with the eye.

29 But do thou become for me a good painter, Lycomedes. Thou hast colours which he giveth thee through me, who painteth all of us

for himself, even Jesus, who knoweth the shapes and appearances and postures and dispositions and types of our souls. And the colours wherewith I bid thee paint are these: faith in God, knowledge, godly fear, friendship, communion, meekness, kindness, brotherly love, purity, simplicity, tranquillity, fearlessness, griefiessness, sobriety, and the whole band of colours that painteth the likeness of thy soul, and even now raiseth up thy members that were cast down, and levelleth them that were lifted up, and tendeth thy bruises, and healeth thy wounds, and ordereth thine hair that was disarranged, and washeth thy face, and chasteneth thine eyes, and purgeth thy bowels, and emptieth thy belly, and cutteth off that which is beneath it; and in a word, when the whole company and mingling of such colours is come together, into thy soul, it shall present it to our Lord Jesus Christ undaunted, whole (unsmoothed), and firm of shape. But this that thou hast now done is childish and imperfect: thou hast drawn a dead likeness of the dead.

There need be no portion of text lost at this point: but possibly some few sentences have been omitted. The transition is abrupt and the new episode has not, as elsewhere, a title of its own.

30 And he commanded Verus (Berus), the brother that ministered to him, to gather the aged women that were in all Ephesus, and made ready, he and Cleopatra and Lycomedes, all things for the care of them. Verus, then, came to John, saying: Of the aged women that are here over threescore years old I have found four only sound in body, and of the rest some . . . . (a word gone) and some palsied and others sick. And when he heard that, John kept silence for a long time, and rubbed his face and said: O the slackness (weakness) of them that dwell in Ephesus! O the state of dissolution, and the weakness toward God! O devil, that hast so long mocked the faithful in Ephesus! Jesus, who giveth me grace and the gift to have my confidence in him, saith to me in silence: Send after the old women that are sick and come (be) with them into the theatre, and through me heal them: for there are some of them that will come unto this spectacle whom by these

healings I will convert and make them useful for some end.

31 Now when all the multitude was come together to Lycomedes, he dismissed them on John's behalf, saying: Tomorrow come ye to the theatre, as many as desire to see the power of God. And the multitude, on the morrow, while it was yet night, came to the theatre: so that the proconsul also heard of it and hasted and took his sent with all the people. And a certain praetor, Andromeus, who was the first of the Ephesians at that time, put it about that John had promised things impossible and incredible: But if, said he, he is able to do any such thing as I hear, let him come into the public theatre, when it is open, naked, and holding nothing in his hands, neither let him name that magical name which I have heard him utter.

32 John therefore, having heard this and being moved by. these words, commanded the aged women to be brought into the theatre: and when they were all brought into the midst, some of them upon beds and others lying in a deep sleep, and all the city had run together, and a great silence was made, John opened his mouth and began to say:

33 Ye men of Ephesus, learn first of all wherefore I am visiting in your city, or what is this great confidence which I have towards you, so that it may become manifest to this general assembly and to all of you (or, so that I manifest myself to). I have been sent, then, upon a mission which is not of man's ordering, and not upon any vain journey; neither am I a merchant that make bargains or exchanges; but Jesus Christ whom I preach, being compassionate and kind, desireth by my means to convert all of you who are held in unbelief and sold unto evil lusts, and to deliver you from error; and by his power will I confound even the unbelief of your praetor, by raising up them that lie before you, whom ye all behold, in what plight and in what sicknesses they are. And to do this (to confound Andronicus) is not possible for me if they perish: therefore shall they be healed.

34 But this first I have desired to sow in your ears, even that ye should take care for your souls -on which account I am come unto

you- and not expect that this time will be for ever, for it is but a moment, and not lay up treasures upon the earth where all things do fade. Neither think that when ye have gotten children ye can rest upon them (?), and try not for their sakes to defraud and overreach. Neither, ye poor, be vexed if ye have not wherewith to minister unto pleasures; for men of substance when they are diseased call you happy. Neither, ye rich, rejoice that ye have much money, for by possessing these things ye provide for yourselves grief that ye cannot be rid of when ye lose them; and besides, while it is with you, ye are afraid lest some one attack you on account of it.

35 Thou also that art puffed up because of the shapeliness of thy body, and art of an high look, shalt see the end of the promise thereof in the grave; and thou that rejoicest in adultery, know that both law and nature avenge it upon thee, and before these, conscience; and thou, adulteress, that art an adversary of the law, knowest not whither thou shalt come in the end. And thou that sharest not with the needy, but hast monies laid up, when thou departest out of this body and hast need of some mercy when thou burnest in fire, shalt have none to pity thee; and thou the wrathful and passionate, know that thy conversation is like the brute beasts; and thou, drunkard and quarreller, learn that thou losest thy senses by being enslaved to a shameful and dirty desire.

36 Thou that rejoicest in gold and delightest thyself with ivory and jewels, when night falleth, canst thou behold what thou lovest? thou that art vanquished by soft raiment, and then leavest life, will those things profit thee in the place whither thou goest? And let the murderer know that the condign punishment is laid up for him twofold after his departure hence. Likewise also thou poisoner, sorcerer, robber, defrauder, sodomite, thief, and as many as are of that band, ye shall come at last, as your works do lead you, unto unquenchable fire, and utter darkness, and the pit of punishment, and eternal threatenings. Wherefore, ye men of Ephesus, turn yourselves, knowing this also, that kings, rulers, tyrants, boasters, and they that

have conquered in wars, stripped of all things when they depart hence, do suffer pain, lodged in eternal misery.

37 And having thus said, John by the power of God healed all the diseases.

This sentence must be an abridgement of a much longer narration. The manuscript indicates no break at this point: but we must suppose a not inconsiderable loss of text. For one thing, Andronicus, who is here an unbeliever, appears as a convert in the next few lines. Now he is, as we shall see later, the husband of an eminent believer, Drusiana; and his and her conversion will have been told at some length; and I do not doubt that among other things there was a discourse of John persuading them to live in continence.

37 (continued.) Now the brethren from Miletus said unto John: We have continued a long time at Ephesus; if it seem good to thee, let us go also to Smyrna; for we hear already that the mighty works of God have reached it also. And Andronicus said to them: Whensoever the teacher willeth, then let us go. But John said: Let us first go unto the temple of Artemis, for perchance there also, if we show ourselves, the servants of the Lord will be found.

38 After two days, then, was the birthday of the idol temple. John therefore, when all were clad in white, alone put on black raiment and went up into the temple. And they took him and essayed to kill him. But John said: Ye are mad to set upon me, a man that is the servant of the only God. And he gat him up upon an high pedestal and said unto them:

39 Ye run hazard, men of Ephesus, of being like in character to the sea: every river that floweth in and every spring that runneth down, and the rains, and waves that press upon each other, and torrents full of rocks are made salt together by the bitter telementt (MS. promise!) that is therein. So ye also remaining unchanged unto this day toward true godliness are become corrupted by your ancient rites of worship. How many wonders and healings of diseases have ye seen wrought through me? And yet are ye blinded in your hearts and cannot

recover sight. What is it, then, O men of Ephesus? I have adventured now and come up even into this your idol temple. I will convict you of being most godless, and dead from the understanding of mankind. Behold, I stand here: ye all say that ye have a goddess, even Artemis: pray then unto her that I alone may die; or else I only, if ye are not able to do this, will call upon mine own god, and for your unbelief I will cause every one of you to die.

40 But they who had beforetime made trial of him and had seen dead men raised up, cried out: Slay us not so, we beseech thee, John. We know that thou canst do it. And John said to them: If then ye desire not to die, let that which ye worship be confounded, and wherefore it is confounded, that ye also may depart from your ancient error. For now is it time that either ye be converted by my God, or I myself die by your goddess; for I will pray in your presence and entreat my God that mercy be shown unto you.

41 And having so said he prayed thus: O God that art God above all that are called gods, that until this day hast been set at nought in the city of the Ephesians; that didst put into my mind to come into this place, whereof I never thought; that dost convict every manner of worship by turning men unto thee; at whose name every idol fleeth and every evil spirit and every unclean power; now also by the flight of the evil spirit here at thy name, even of him that deceiveth this great multitude, show thou thy mercy in this place, for they have been made to err.

42 And as John spake these things, immediately the altar of Artemis was parted into many pieces, and all the things that were dedicated in the temple fell, and [MS. that which seemed good to him] was rent asunder, and likewise of the images of the gods more than seven. And the half of the temple fell down, so that the priest was slain at one blow by the falling of the (?roof, ? beam). The multitude of the Ephesians therefore cried out: One is the God of John, one is the God that hath pity on us, for thou only art God: now are we turned to thee, beholding thy marvellous works! have mercy

on us, O God, according to thy will, and save us from our great error! And some of them, lying on their faces, made supplication, and some kneeled and besought, and some rent their clothes and wept, and others tried to escape.

43 But John spread forth his hands, and being uplifted in soul, said unto the Lord: Glory be to thee, my Jesus, the only God of truth, for that thou dost gain (receive) thy servants by divers devices. And having so said, he said to the people: Rise up from the floor, ye men of Ephesus, and pray to my God, and recognize the invisible power that cometh to manifestation, and the wonderful works which are wrought before your eyes. Artemis ought to have succoured herself: her servant ought to have been helped of her and not to have died. Where is the power of the evil spirit? where are her sacrifices? where her birthdays? where her festivals? where are the garlands? where is all that sorcery and the poisoning (witchcraft) that is sister thereto?

44 But the people rising up from off the floor went hastily and cast down the rest of the idol temple, crying: The God of John only do we know, and him hereafter do we worship, since he hath had mercy upon us! And as John came down from thence, much people took hold of him, saying: Help us, O John! Assist us that do perish in vain! Thou seest our purpose: thou seest the multitude following thee and hanging upon thee in hope toward thy God. We have seen the way wherein we went astray when we lost him: we have seen our gods that were set up in vain: we have seen the great and shameful derision that is come to them: but suffer us, we pray thee, to come unto thine house and to be succoured without hindrance. Receive us that are in bewilderment.

45 And John said to them: Men (of Ephesus), believe that for your sakes I have continued in Ephesus, and have put off my journey unto Smyrna and to the rest of the cities, that there also the servants of Christ may turn to him. But since I am not yet perfectly assured concerning you, I have continued praying to my God and beseeching him that I should then depart from Ephesus when I have confirmed

you in the faith: and whereas I see that this is come to pass and yet
more is being fulfilled, I will not leave you until I have weaned you
like children from the nurse's milk, and have set you upon a firm
rock.

46 John therefore continued with them, receiving them in the
house of Andromeus. And one of them that were gathered laid down
the dead body of the priest of Artemis before the door [of the temple],
for he was his kinsman, and came in quickly with the rest, saying
nothing of it. John, therefore, after the discourse to the brethren, and
the prayer and the thanksgiving (eucharist) and the laying of hands
upon every one of the congregation, said by the spirit: There is one
here who moved by faith in God hath laid down the priest of Artemis
before the gate and is come in, and in the yearning of his soul, taking
care first for himself, hath thought thus in himself: It is better for me
to take thought for the living than for my kinsman that is dead: for I
know that if I turn to the Lord and save mine own soul, John will not
deny to raise up the dead also. And John arising from his place went
to that into which that kinsman of the priest who had so thought was
entered, and took him by the hand and said: Hadst thou this thought
when thou camest unto me, my child? And he, taken with trembling
and affright, said: Yes, lord, and cast himself at his feet. And John
said: Our Lord is Jesus Christ, who will show his power in thy dead
kinsman by raising him up.

47 And he made the young man rise, and took his hand and said:
It is no great matter for a man that is master of great mysteries to
continue wearying himself over small things: or what great thing is it
to rid men of diseases of the body? And yet holding the young man by
the hand he said: I say unto thee, child, go and raise the dead thyself,
saying nothing but this only: John the servant of God saith to thee,
Arise. And the young man went to his kinsman and said this only
-and much people was with him- and entered in unto John, bringing
him alive. And John, when he saw him that was raised, said: Now
that thou art raised, thou dost not truly live, neither art partaker or

heir of the true life: wilt thou belong unto him by whose name and power thou wast raised? And now believe, and thou shall live unto all ages. And he forthwith believed upon the Lord Jesus and thereafter clave unto John.

[Another manuscript (Q. Paris Gr. 1468, of the eleventh century) has another form of this story. John destroys the temple of Artemis, and then 'we' go to Smyrna and all the idols are broken: Bucolus, Polycarp, and Andronicus are left to preside over the district. There were there two priests of Artemis, brothers, and one died. The raising is told much as in the older text, but more shortly.

'We' remained four years in the region, which was wholly converted, and then returned to Ephesus.]

48 Now on the next day John, having seen in a dream that he must walk three miles outside the gates, neglected it not, but rose up early and set out upon the way, together with the brethren.

And a certain countryman who was admonished by his father not to take to himself the wife of a fellow labourer of his who threatened to kill him -this young man would not endure the admonition of his father, but kicked him and left him without speech (sc. dead). And John, seeing what had befallen, said unto the Lord: Lord, was it on this account that thou didst bid me come out hither to-day?

49 But the young man, beholding the violence (sharpness) of death, and looking to be taken, drew out the sickle that was in his girdle and started to run to his own abode; and John met him and said: Stand still, thou most shameless devil, and tell me whither thou runnest bearing a sickle that thirsteth for blood. And the young man was troubled and cast the iron on the ground, and said to him: I have done a wretched and barbarous deed and I know it, and so I determined to do an evil yet worse and more cruel, even to die myself at once. For because my father was alway curbing me to sobriety, that I should live without adultery, and chastely, I could not endure him to reprove me, and I kicked him and slew him, and when I saw what was done, I was hasting to the woman for whose sake I became my

father's murderer, with intent to kill her and her husband, and myself last of all: for I could not bear to be seen of the husband of the woman, and undergo the judgement of death.

50 And John said to him: That I may not by going away and leaving you in danger give place to him that desireth to laugh and sport with thee, come thou with me and show me thy father, where he lieth. And if I raise him up for thee, wilt thou hereafter abstain from the woman that is become a snare to thee. And the young man said: If thou raisest up my father himself for me alive, and if I see him whole and continuing in life, I will hereafter abstain from her.

51 And while he was speaking, they came to the place where the old man lay dead, and many passers-by were standing near thereto. And John said to the youth: Thou wretched man, didst thou not spare even the old age of thy father? And he, weeping and tearing his hair, said that he repented thereof; and John the servant of the Lord said: Thou didst show me I was to set forth for this place, thou knewest that this would come to pass, from whom nothing can be hid of things done in life, that givest me power to work every cure and healing by thy will: now also give me this old man alive, for thou seest that his murderer is become his own judge: and spare him, thou only Lord, that spared not his father (because he) counselled him for the best.

52 And with these words he came near to the old man and said: My Lord will not be weak to spread out his kind pity and his condescending mercy even unto thee: rise up therefore and give glory to God for the work that is come to pass at this moment. And the old man said: I arise, Lord. And he rose and sat up and said: I was released from a terrible life and had to bear the insults of my son, dreadful and many, and his want of natural affection, and to what end hast thou called me back, O man of the living God? (And John answered him: If) thou art raised only for the same end, it were better for thee to die; but raise thyself unto better things. And he took him and led him into the city, preaching unto him the grace of God, so

that before he entered the gate the old man believed.

53 But the young man, when he beheld the unlooked-for raising of his father, and the saving of himself, took a sickle and mutilated himself, and ran to the house wherein he had his adulteress, and reproached her, saying: For thy sake I became the murderer of my father and of you two and of myself: there thou hast that which is alike guilty of all. For on me God hath had mercy, that I should know his power.

54 And he came back and told John in presence of the brethren what he had done. But John said to him: He that put it into thine heart, young man, to kill thy father and become the adulterer of another man's wife, the same made thee think it a right deed to take away also the unruly members. But thou shouldest have done away, not with the place of sin, but the thought which through those members showed itself harmful: for it is not the instruments that are injurious, but the unseen springs by which every shameful emotion is stirred and cometh to light. Repent therefore, my child, of this fault, and having learnt the wiles of Satan thou shalt have God to help thee in all the necessities of thy soul. And the young man kept silence and attended, having repented of his former sins, that he should obtain pardon from the goodness of God: and he did not separate from John.

55 When, then, these things had been done by him in the city of the Ephesians, they of Smyrna sent unto him saying: We hear that the God whom thou preachest is not envious, and hath charged thee not to show partiality by abiding in one place. Since, then, thou art a preacher of such a God, come unto Smyrna and unto the other cities, that we may come to know thy God, and having known him may have our hope in him.

[Q has the above story also, and continues with an incident which is also quoted in a different form (and not as from these Acts) by John Cassian. Q has it thus:

Now one day as John was seated, a partridge flew by and came and played in the dust before him; and John looked on it and wondered.

And a certain priest came, who was one of his hearers, and came to John and saw the partridge playing in the dust before him, and was offended in himself and said: Can such and so great a man take pleasure in a partridge playing in the dust? But John perceiving in the spirit the thought of him, said to him: It were better for thee also, my child, to look at a partridge playing in the dust and not to defile thyself with shameful and profane practices: for he who awaiteth the conversion and repentance of all men hath brought thee here on this account: for I have no need of a partridge playing in the dust. For the partridge is thine own soul.

Then the elder, hearing this and seeing that he was not bidden, but that the apostle of Christ had told him all that was in his heart, fell on his face on the earth and cried aloud, saying: Now know I that God dwelleth in thee, O blessed John! for he that tempteth thee tempteth him that cannot be tempted. And he entreated him to pray for him. And he instructed him and delivered him the rules (canons) and let him go to his house, glorifying God that is over all.

Cassian, Collation XXIV. 21, has it thus:

It is told that the most blessed Evangelist John, when he was gently stroking a partridge with his hands, suddenly saw one in the habit of a hunter coming to him. He wondered that a man of such repute and fame should demean himself to such small and humble amusements, and said: Art thou that John whose eminent and widespread fame hath enticed me also with great desire to know thee? Why then art thou taken up with such mean amusements? The blessed John said to him: What is that which thou carriest in thy hands? A bow, said he. And why, said he, dost thou not bear it about always stretched? He answered him: I must not, lest by constant bending the strength of its vigour be wrung and grow soft and perish, and when there is need that the arrows be shot with much strength at some beast, the strength being lost by excess of continual tension, a forcible blow cannot be dealt. Just so, said the blessed John, let not this little and brief relaxation of my mind offend thee, young man, for

unless it doth sometimes ease and relax by some remission the force
of its tension, it will grow slack through unbroken rigour and will not
be able to obey the power of the Spirit.

The only common point of the two stories is that St. John amuses
himself with a partridge, and a spectator thinks it unworthy of him.
The two morals differ wholly. The amount of text lost here is of quite
uncertain length. It must have told of the doings at Smyrna, and also,
it appears, at Laodicca (see the title of the next section). One of the
episodes must have been the conversion of a woman of evil life (see
below, 'the harlot that was chaste ')—]

Our best manuscript prefixes a title to the next section:

From Laodicca to Ephesus the second time.

58 Now when some long time had passed, and none of the
brethren had been at any time grieved by John, they were then
grieved because he had said: Brethren, it is now time for me to go to
Ephesus (for so have I agreed with them that dwell there) lest they
become slack, now for a long time having no man to confirm them.
But all of you must have your minds steadfast towards God, who
never forsaketh us.

But when they heard this from him, the brethren lamented
because they were to be parted from him. And John said: Even if I be
parted from you, yet Christ is always with you: whom if ye love purely
ye will have his fellowship without reproach, for if he be loved, he
preventeth (anticipateth) them that love him.

59 And having so said, and bidden farewell to them, and left much
money with the brethren for distribution, he went forth unto Ephesus,
while all the brethren lamented and groaned. And there accompanied
him, of Ephesus, both Andronicus and Drusiana and Lycomedes and
Cleobius and their families. And there followed him Aristobula also,
who had heard that her husband Tertullus had died on the way, and
Aristippus with Xenophon, and the harlot that was chaste, and many
others, whom he exhorted at all times to cleave to the Lord, and they
would no more be parted from him.

60 Now on the first day we arrived at a deserted inn, and when we were at a loss for a bed for John, we saw a droll matter. There was one bedstead lying somewhere there without coverings, whereon we spread the cloaks which we were wearing, and we prayed him to lie down upon it and rest, while the rest of us all slept upon the floor. But he when he lay down was troubled by the bugs, and as they continued to become yet more troublesome to him, when it was now about the middle of the night, in the hearing of us all he said to them: I say unto you, O bugs, behave yourselves, one and all, and leave your abode for this night and remain quiet in one place, and keep your distance from the servants of God. And as we laughed, and went on talking for some time, John addressed himself to sleep; and we, talking low, gave him no disturbance (or, thanks to him we were not disturbed).

61 But when the day was now dawning I arose first, and with me Verus and Andronicus, and we saw at the door of the house which we had taken a great number of bugs standing, and while we wondered at the great sight of them, and all the brethren were roused up because of them, John continued sleeping. And when he was awaked we declared to him what we had seen. And he sat up on the bed and looked at them and said: Since ye have well behaved yourselves in hearkening to my rebuke, come unto your place. And when he had said this, and risen from the bed, the bugs running from the door hasted to the bed and climbed up by the legs thereof and disappeared into the joints. And John said again: This creature hearkened unto the voice of a man, and abode by itself and was quiet and trespassed not; but we which hear the voice and commandments of God disobey and are light-minded: and for how long?

62 After these things we came to Ephesus: and the brethren there, who had for a long time known that John was coming, ran together to the house of Andronicus (where also he came to lodge), handling his feet and laying their hands upon their own faces and kissing them (and many rejoiced even to touch his vesture, and were healed by touching the clothes of the holy apostle. [So the Latin, which has this

section; the Greek has: so that they even touched his garments).]

63 And whereas there was great love and joy unsurpassed among the brethren, a certain one, a messenger of Satan, became enamoured of Drusiana, though he saw and knew that she was the wife of Andronicus. To whom many said: It is not possible for thee to obtain that woman, seeing that for a long time she has even separated herself from her husband for godliness' sake. Art thou only ignorant that Andronicus, not being aforetime that which now he is, a God-fearing man, shut her up in a tomb, saying: Either I must have thee as the wife whom I had before, or thou shalt die. And she chose rather to die than to do that foulness. If, then, she would not consent, for godliness' sake, to cohabit with her lord and husband, but even persuaded him to be of the same mind as herself, will she consent to thee desiring to be her seducer? depart from this madness which hath no rest in thee: give up this deed which thou canst not bring to accomplishment.

64 But his familiar friends saying these things to him did not convince him, but with shamelessness he courted her with messages; and when he learnt the insults and disgraces which she returned, he spent his life in melancholy (or better, she, when she learnt of this disgrace and insult at his hand, spent her life in heaviness). And after two days Drusiana took to her bed from heaviness, and was in a fever and said: Would that I had not now come home to my native place, I that have become an offence to a man ignorant of godliness! for if it were one who was filled with the word of God, he would not have gone to such a pitch of madness. But now (therefore) Lord, since I am become the occasion of a blow unto a soul devoid of knowledge, set me free from this chain and remove me unto thee quickly. And in the presence of John, who knew nothing at all of such a matter, Drusiana departed out of life not wholly happy, yea, even troubled because of the spiritual hurt of the man.

65 But Andronicus, grieved with a secret grief, mourned in his soul, and wept openly, so that John checked him often and said to him: Upon a better hope hath Drusiana removed out of this

unrighteous life. And Andronicus answered him: Yea, I am persuaded of it, O John, and I doubt not at all in regard of trust in my God: but this very thing do I hold fast, that she departed out of life pure.

66 And when she was carried forth, John took hold on Andronicus, and now that he knew the cause, he mourned more than Andronicus. And he kept silence, considering the provocation of the adversary, and for a space sat still. Then, the brethren being gathered there to hear what word he would speak of her that was departed, he began to say:

67 When the pilot that voyageth, together with them that sail with him, and the ship herself, arriveth in a calm and stormless harbour, then let him say that he is safe. And the husbandman that hath committed the seed to the earth, and toiled much in the care and protection of it, let him then take rest from his labours, when he layeth up the seed with manifold increase in his barns. Let him that enterpriseth to run in the course, then exult when he beareth home the prize. Let him that inscribeth his name for the boxing, then boast himself when he receiveth the crowns: and so in succession is it with all contests and crafts, when they do not fail in the end, but show themselves to be like that which they promised (corrupt).

68 And thus also I think is it with the faith which each one of us practiseth, that it is then discerned whether it be indeed true, when it continueth like itself even until the end of life. For many obstacles fall into the way, and prepare disturbance for the minds of men: care, children, parents, glory, poverty, flattery, prime of life, beauty, conceit, lust, wealth, anger, uplifting, slackness, envy, jealousy, neglect, fear, insolence, love, deceit, money, pretence, and other such obstacles, as many as there are in this life: as also the pilot sailing a prosperous course is opposed by the onset of contrary winds and a great storm and mighty waves out of calm, and the husbandman by untimely winter and blight and creeping things rising out of the earth, and they that strive in the games 'just do not win', and they that exercise crafts

are hindered by the divers difficulties of them.

69 But before all things it is needful that the believer should look before at his ending and understand it in what manner it will come upon him, whether it will be vigorous and sober and without any obstacle, or disturbed and clinging to the things that are here, and bound down by desires. So is it right that a body should be praised as comely when it is wholly stripped, and a general as great when he hath accomplished every promise of the war, and a physician as excellent when he hath succeeded in every cure, and a soul as full of faith and worthy (or receptive) of God when it hath paid its promise in full: not that soul which began well and was dissolved into all the things of this life and fell away, nor that which is numb, having made an effort to attain to better things, and then is borne down to temporal things, nor that which hath longed after the things of time more than those of eternity, nor that which exchangeth [enduring for things] those that endure not, nor that which hath honoured the works of dishonour that deserve shame, nor that which taketh pledges of Satan, nor that which hath received the serpent into its own house, nor that which suffereth reproach for God's sake and then is [not] ashamed, nor that which with the mouth saith yea, but indeed approveth not itself: but that which hath prevailed not to be made weak by foul pleasure, not to be overcome by light-mindedness, not to be caught by the bait of love of money, not to be betrayed by vigour of body or wrath.

70 And as John was discoursing yet further unto the brethren that they should despise temporal things in respect of the eternal, he that was enamoured of Drusiana, being inflamed with an horrible lust and possession of the many-shaped Satan, bribed the steward of Andronicus who was a lover of money with a great sum: and he opened the tomb and gave him opportunity to wreak the forbidden thing upon the dead body. Not having succeeded with her when alive, he was still importunate after her death to her body, and said: If thou wouldst not have to do with me while thou livedst, I will

outrage thy corpse now thou art dead. With this design, and having managed for himself the wicked act by means of the abominable steward, he rushed with him to the sepulchre; they opened the door and began to strip the grave-clothes from the corpse, saying: What art thou profited, poor Drusiana? couldest thou not have done this in life, which perchance would not have grieved thee, hadst thou done it willingly?

71 And as these men were speaking thus, and only the accustomed shift now remained on her body, a strange spectacle was seen, such as they deserve to suffer who do such deeds. A serpent appeared from some quarter and dealt the steward a single bite and slew him: but the young man it did not strike; but coiled about his feet, hissing terribly, and when he fell mounted on his body and sat upon him.

72 Now on the next day John came, accompanied by Andronicus and the brethren, to the sepulchre at dawn, it being now the third day from Drusiana's death, that we might break bread there. And first, when they set out, the keys were sought for and could not be found; but John said to Andronicus: It is quite right that they should be lost, for Drusiana is not in the sepulchre; nevertheless, let us go, that thou mayest not be neglectful, and the doors shall be opened of themselves, even as the Lord hath done for us many such things.

73 And when we were at the place, at the commandment of the master, the doors were opened, and we saw by the tomb of Drusiana a beautiful youth, smiling: and John, when he saw him, cried out and said: Art thou come before us hither too, beautiful one? and for what cause? And we heard a voice saying to him: For Drusiana's sake, whom thou art to raise up-for I was within a little of finding her [shamed] - and for his sake that lieth dead beside her tomb. And when the beautiful one had said this unto John he went up into the heavens in the sight of us all. And John, turning to the other side of the sepulchre, saw a young man-even Callimachus, one of the chief of the Ephesians-and a huge serpent sleeping upon him, and the

steward of Andronicus, Fortunatus by name, lying dead. And at the
sight of the two he stood perplexed, saying to the brethren: What
meaneth such a sight? or wherefore hath not the Lord declared unto
me what was done here, he who hath never neglected me?

74 And Andronicus seeing those corpses, leapt up and went to
Drusiana's tomb, and seeing her lying in her shift only, said to John:
I understand what has happened, thou blessed servant of God, John.
This Callimachus was enamoured of my sister; and because he never
won her, though he often assayed it, he hath bribed this mine
accursed steward with a great sum, perchance designing, as now we
may see, to fulfil by his means the tragedy of his conspiracy, for indeed
Callimachus avowed this to many, saying: If she will not consent to
me when living, she shall be outraged when dead. And it may be,
master, that the beautiful one knew it and suffered not her body to be
insulted, and therefore have these died who made that attempt. And
can it be that the voice that said unto thee, 'Raise up Drusiana',
foreshowed this? because she departed out of this life in sorrow of
mind. But I believe him that said that this is one of the men that have
gone astray; for thou wast bidden to raise him up: for as to the other,
I know that he is unworthy of salvation. But this one thing I beg of
thee: raise up Callimachus first, and he will confess to us what is come
about.

75 And John, looking upon the body, said to the venomous beast:
Get thee away from him that is to be a servant of Jesus Christ; and
stood up and prayed over him thus: O God whose name is glorified by
us, as of right: O God who subduest every injurious force: O God
whose will is accomplished, who alway hearest us: now also let thy gift
be accomplished in this young man; and if there be any dispensation
to be wrought through him, manifest it unto us when he is raised up.
And straightway the young man rose up, and for a whole hour kept
silence.

76 But when he came to his right senses, John asked of him about
his entry into the sepulchre, what it meant, and learning from him

that which Andronicus had told him, namely, that he was enamoured of Drusiana, John inquired of him again if he had fulfilled his foul intent, to insult a body full of holiness. And he answered him: How could I accomplish it when this fearful beast struck down Fortunatus at a blow in my sight: and rightly, since he encouraged my frenzy, when I was already cured of that unreasonable and horrible madness: but me it stopped with affright, and brought me to that plight in which ye saw me before I arose. And another thing yet more wondrous I will tell thee, which yet went nigh to slay and was within a little of making me a corpse. When my soul was stirred up with folly and the uncontrollable malady was troubling me, and I had now torn away the grave-clothes in which she was clad, and I had then come out of the grave and laid them as thou seest, I went again to my unholy work: and I saw a beautiful youth covering her with his mantle, and from his eyes sparks of light came forth unto her eyes; and he uttered words to me, saying: Callimachus, die that thou mayest live. Now who he was I knew not, O servant of God; but that now thou hast appeared here, I recognize that he was an angel of God, that I know well; and this I know of a truth that it is a true God that is proclaimed by thee, and of it I am persuaded. But I beseech thee, be not slack to deliver me from this calamity and this fearful crime, and to present me unto thy God as a man deceived with a shameful and foul deceit. Beseeching help therefore of thee, I take hold on thy feet. I would become one of them that hope in Christ, that the voice may prove true which said to me, 'Die that thou mayest live': and that voice hath also fulfilled its effect, for he is dead, that faithless, disorderly, godless one, and I have been raised by thee, I who will be faithful, God-fearing, knowing the truth, which I entreat thee may be shown me by thee.

77 And John, filled with great gladness and perceiving the whole spectacle of the salvation of man, said: What thy power is, Lord Jesu Christ, I know not, bewildered as I am at thy much compassion and boundless long-suffering. O what a greatness that came down into

bondage! O unspeakable liberty brought into slavery by us! O incomprehensible glory that is come unto us! thou that hast kept the dead tabernacle safe from insult; that hast redeemed the man that stained himself with blood and chastened the soul of him that would defile the corruptible body; Father that hast had pity and compassion on the man that cared not for thee; We glorify thee, and praise and bless and thank thy great goodness and long-suffering, O holy Jesu, for thou only art God, and none else: whose is the might that cannot be conspired against, now and world without end. Amen.

78 And when he had said this John took Callimachus and saluted (kissed) him, saying: Glory be to our God, my child, who hath had mercy on thee, and made me worthy to glorify his power, and thee also by a good course to depart from that thine abominable madness and drunkenness, and hath called thee unto his own rest and unto renewing of life.

79 But Andronicus, beholding the dead Callimachus raised, besought John, with the brethren, to raise up Drusiana also, saying: O John, let Drusiana arise and spend happily that short space (of life) which she gave up through grief about Callimachus, when she thought she had become a stumbling block to him: and when the Lord will, he shall take her again to himself. And John without delay went unto her tomb and took her hand and said: Upon thee that art the only God do I call, the more than great, the unutterable, the incomprehensible: unto whom every power of principalities is subjected: unto whom all authority boweth: before whom all pride falleth down and keepeth silence: whom devils hearing of tremble: whom all creation perceiving keepeth its bounds. Let thy name be glorified by us, and raise up Drusiana, that Callimachus may yet more be confirmed unto thee who dispensest that which unto men is without a way and impossible, but to thee only possible, even salvation and resurrection: and that Drusiana may now come forth in peace, having about her not any the least hindrance -now that the young man is turned unto thee- in her course toward thee.

80 And after these words John said unto Drusiana: Drusiana, arise. And she arose and came out of the tomb; and when she saw herself in her shift only, she was perplexed at the thing, and learned the whole accurately from Andronicus, the while John lay upon his face, and Callimachus with voice and tears glorified God, and she also rejoiced, glorifying him in like manner.

81 And when she had clothed herself, she turned and saw Fortunatus lying, and said unto John: Father, let this man also rise, even if he did assay to become my betrayer. But Callimachus, when he heard her say that, said: Do not, I beseech thee, Drusiana, for the voice which I heard took no thought of him, but declared concerning thee only, and I saw and believed: for if he had been good, perchance God would have had mercy on him also and would have raised him by means of the blessed John: he knew therefore that the man was come to a bad end [Lat. he judged him worthy to die whom he did not declare worthy to rise again]. And John said to him: We have not learned, my child, to render evil for evil: for God, though we have done much ill and no good toward him, hath not given retribution unto us, but repentance, and though we were ignorant of his name he did not neglect us but had mercy on us, and when we blasphemed him, he did not punish but pitied us, and when we disbelieved him he bore us no grudge, and when we persecuted his brethren he did not recompense us evil but put into our minds repentance and abstinence from evil, and exhorted us to come unto him, as he hath thee also, my son Callimachus, and not remembering thy former evil hath made thee his servant, waiting upon his mercy. Wherefore if thou allowest not me to raise up Fortunatus, it is for Drusiana so to do.

82 And she, delaying not, went with rejoicing of spirit and soul unto the body of Fortunatus and said: Jesu Christ, God of the ages, God of truth, that hast granted me to see wonders and signs, and given to me to become partaker of thy name; that didst breathe thyself into me with thy many-shaped countenance, and hadst mercy on me in many ways; that didst protect me by thy great goodness

when I was oppressed by Andronicus that was of old my husband; that didst give me thy servant Andronicus to be my brother; that hast kept me thine handmaid pure unto this day; that didst raise me up by thy servant John, and when I was raised didst show me him that was made to stumble free from stumbling; that hast given me perfect rest in thee, and lightened me of the secret madness; whom I have loved and affectioned: I pray thee, O Christ, refuse not thy Drusiana that asketh thee to raise up Fortunatus, even though he assayed to become my betrayer.

83 And taking the hand of the dead man she said: Rise up, Fortunatus, in the name of our Lord Jesus Christ. And Fortunatus arose, and when he saw John in the sepulchre, and Andronicus, and Drusiana raised from the dead, and Callimachus a believer, and the rest of the brethren glorifying God, he said: O, to what have the powers of these clever men attained! I did not want to be raised, but would rather die, so as not to see them. And with these words he fled and went out of the sepulchre.

84 And John, when he saw the unchanged mind (soul) of Fortunatus, said: O nature that is not changed for the better! O fountain of the soul that abideth in foulness! O essence of corruption full of darkness! O death exulting in them that are thine! O fruitless tree full of fire! O tree that bearest coals for fruit! O matter that dwellest with the madness of matter (al. O wood of trees full of unwholesome shoots) and neighbour of unbelief! Thou hast proved who thou art, and thou art always convicted, with thy children. And thou knowest not how to praise the better things: for thou hast them not. Therefore, such as is thy way (?fruit), such also is thy root and thy nature. Be thou destroyed from among them that trust in the Lord: from their thoughts, from their mind, from their souls, from their bodies, from their acts) their life, their conversation, from their business, their occupations, their counsel, from the resurrection unto (or rest in) God, from their sweet savour wherein thou wilt [not] share, from their faith, their prayers, from the holy bath, from the

eucharist, from the food of the flesh, from drink, from clothing, from love, from care, from abstinence, from righteousness: from all these, thou most unholy Satan, enemy of God, shall Jesus Christ our God and [the judge] of all that are like thee and have thy character, make thee to perish.

85 And having thus said, John prayed, and took bread and bare it into the sepulchre to break it; and said: We glorify thy name, which converteth us from error and ruthless deceit: we glorify thee who hast shown before our eyes that which we have seen: we bear witness to thy loving-kindness which appeareth in divers ways: we praise thy merciful name, O Lord (we thank thee), who hast convicted them that are convicted of thee: we give thanks to thee, O Lord Jesu Christ, that we are persuaded of thy [grace] which is unchanging: we give thanks to thee who hadst need of our nature that should be saved: we give thanks to thee that hast given us this sure [faith], for thou art [god] alone, both now and ever. We thy servants give thee thanks, O holy one, who are assembled with [good] intent and are gathered out of the world (or risen from death).

86 And having so prayed and given glory to God, he went out of the sepulchre after imparting unto all the brethren of the eucharist of the Lord. And when he was come unto Andronicus' house he said to the brethren: Brethren, a spirit within me hath divined that Fortunatus is about to die of blackness (poisoning of the blood) from the bite of the serpent; but let some one go quickly and learn if it is so indeed. And one of the young men ran and found him dead and the blackness spreading over him, and it had reached his heart: and came and told John that he had been dead three hours. And John said: Thou hast thy child, O devil.

'John therefore was with the brethren rejoicing in the Lord.' This sentence is in the best manuscript. In Bonnet's edition It introduces the last section of the Acts, which follows immediately in the manuscript. It may belong to either episode. The Latin has: And that day he spent joyfully with the brethren.

There cannot be much of a gap between this and the next section, which is perhaps the most interesting in the Acts.

The greater part of this episode is preserved only in one very corrupt fourteenth-century manuscript at Vienna. Two important passages (93-5 (part) and 97-8 (part)) were read at the Second Nicene Council and are preserved in the Acts thereof: a few lines of the Hymn are also cited in Latin by Augustine (Ep. 237 (253) to Ceretius): he found it current separately among the Priscillianists. The whole discourse is the best popular exposition we have of the Docetic view of our Lord's person.

87 Those that were present inquired the cause, and were especially perplexed, because Drusiana had said: The Lord appeared unto me in the tomb in the likeness of John, and in that of a youth. Forasmuch, therefore, as they were perplexed and were, in a manner, not yet stablished in the faith, so as to endure it steadfastly, John said (or John bearing it patiently, said):

88 Men and brethren, ye have suffered nothing strange or incredible as concerning your perception of the [lord], inasmuch as we also, whom he chose for himself to be apostles, were tried in many ways: I, indeed, am neither able to set forth unto you nor to write the things which I both saw and heard: and now is it needful that I should fit them for your hearing; and according as each of you is able to contain it I will impart unto you those things whereof ye are able to become hearers, that ye may see the glory that is about him, which was and is, both now and for ever.

For when he had chosen Peter and Andrew, which were brethren, he cometh unto me and James my brother, saying: I have need of you, come unto me. And my brother hearing that, said: John, what would this child have that is upon the sea-shore and called us? And I said: What child? And he said to me again: That which beckoneth to us. And I answered: Because of our long watch we have kept at sea, thou seest not aright, my brother James; but seest thou not the man that standeth there, comely and fair and of a cheerful countenance? But he said to me: Him I see not, brother; but let us go forth and we shall see what he would have.

89 And so when we had brought the ship to land, we saw him also helping along with us to settle the ship: and when we departed from that place, being minded to follow him, again he was seen of me as having rather bald, but the beard thick and flowing, but of James as a youth whose beard was newly come. We were therefore perplexed, both of us, as to what that which we had seen should mean. And after that, as we followed him, both of us were by little and little [yet more] perplexed as we considered the matter. Yet unto me there then appeared this yet more wonderful thing: for I would try to see him privily, and I never at any time saw his eyes closing (winking), but only open. And oft-times he would appear to me as a small man and uncomely, and then againt as one reaching unto heaven. Also there was in him another marvel: when I sat at meat he would take me upon his own breast; and sometimes his breast was felt of me to be smooth and tender, and sometimes hard like unto stones, so that I was perplexed in myself and said: Wherefore is this so unto me? And as I considered this, he . .

90 And at another time he taketh with him me and James and Peter unto the mountain where he was wont to pray, and we saw in him a light such as it is not possible for a man that useth corruptible (mortal) speech to describe what it was like. Again in like manner he bringeth us three up into the mountain, saying: Come ye with me. And we went again: and we saw him at a distance praying. I, therefore, because he loved me, drew nigh unto him softly, as though he could not see me, and stood looking upon his hinder parts: and I saw that he was not in any wise clad with garments, but was seen of us naked, and not in any wise as a man, and that his feet were whiter than any snow, so that the earth there was lighted up by his feet, and that his head touched the heaven: so that I was afraid and cried out, and he, turning about, appeared as a man of small stature, and caught hold on my beard and pulled it and said to me: John, be not

faithless but believing, and not curious. And I said unto him: But what have I done, Lord? And I say unto you, brethren, I suffered so great pain in that place where he took hold on my beard for thirty days, that I said to him: Lord, if thy twitch when thou wast in sport hath given me so great pain, what were it if thou hadst given me a buffet? And he said unto me: Let it be thine henceforth not to tempt him that cannot be tempted.

91 But Peter and James were wroth because I spake with the Lord, and beckoned unto me that I should come unto them and leave the Lord alone. And I went, and they both said unto me: He (the old man) that was speaking with the Lord upon the top of the mount, who was he? for we heard both of them speaking. And I, having in mind his great grace, and his unity which hath many faces, and his wisdom which without ceasing looketh upon us, said: That shall ye learn if ye inquire of him.

92 Again, once when all we his disciples were at Gennesaret sleeping in one house, I alone having wrapped myself in my mantle, watched (or watched from beneath my mantle) what he should do: and first I heard him say: John, go thou to sleep. And I thereon feigning to sleep saw another like unto him [sleeping], whom also I heard say unto my Lord: Jesus, they whom thou hast chosen believe not yet on thee (or do they not yet, &c.?). And my Lord said unto him: Thou sayest well: for they are men.

93 Another glory also will I tell you, brethren: Sometimes when I would lay hold on him, I met with a material and solid body, and at other times, again, when I felt him, the substance was immaterial and as if it existed not at all. And if at any time he were bidden by some one of the Pharisees and went to the bidding, we went with him, and there was set before each one of us a loaf by them that had bidden us, and with us he also received one; and his own he would bless and part it among us: and of that little every one was filled, and our own loaves were saved whole, so that they which bade him were amazed. And oftentimes when I walked with him, I desired to see the print of his

foot, whether it appeared on the earth; for I saw him as it were lifting himself up from the earth: and I never saw it. And these things I speak unto you, brethren, for the encouragement of your faith toward him; for we must at the present keep silence concerning his mighty and wonderful works, inasmuch as they are unspeakable and, it may be, cannot at all be either uttered or heard.

94 Now before he was taken by the lawless Jews, who also were governed by (had their law from) the lawless serpent, he gathered all of us together and said: Before I am delivered up unto them let us sing an hymn to the Father, and so go forth to that which lieth before us. He bade us therefore make as it were a ring, holding one another's hands, and himself standing in the midst he said: Answer Amen unto me. He began, then, to sing an hymn and to say:

Glory be to thee, Father.

And we, going about in a ring, answered him: Amen.

Glory be to thee, Word: Glory be to thee, Grace. Amen.

Glory be to thee, Spirit: Glory be to thee, Holy One:

Glory be to thy glory. Amen.

We praise thee, O Father; we give thanks to thee, O Light, wherein darkness

dwelleth not. Amen.

95 Now whereas (or wherefore) we give thanks, I say:

I would be saved, and I would save. Amen.

I would be loosed, and I would loose. Amen.

I would be wounded, and I would wound. Amen.

I would be born, and I would bear. Amen.

I would eat, and I would be eaten. Amen.

I would hear, and I would be heard. Amen.

I would be thought, being wholly thought. Amen.

I would be washed, and I would wash. Amen.

Grace danceth. I would pipe; dance ye all. Amen.

I would mourn: lament ye all. Amen.

The number Eight (lit. one ogdoad) singeth praise with us. Amen.

The number Twelve danceth on high. Amen.

The Whole on high hath part in our dancing. Amen.

Whoso danceth not, knoweth not what cometh to pass. Amen.

I would flee, and I would stay. Amen.

I would adorn, and I would be adorned. Amen.

I would be united, and I would unite. Amen.

A house I have not, and I have houses. Amen.

A place I have not, and I have places. Amen.

A temple I have not, and I have temples. Amen.

A lamp am I to thee that beholdest me. Amen.

A mirror am I to thee that perceivest me. Amen.

A door am I to thee that knockest at me. Amen.

A way am I to thee a wayfarer. [amen].

96 Now answer thou (or as thou respondest) unto my dancing. Behold thyself in me who speak, and seeing what I do, keep silence about my mysteries.

Thou that dancest, perceive what I do, for thine is this passion of the manhood, which I am about to suffer. For thou couldest not at all have understood what thou sufferest if I had not been sent unto thee, as the word of the Father. Thou that sawest what I suffer sawest me as suffering, and seeing it thou didst not abide but wert wholly moved, moved to make wise. Thou hast me as a bed, rest upon me. Who I am, thou shalt know when I depart. What now I am seen to be, that I am not. Thou shalt see when thou comest. If thou hadst known how to suffer, thou wouldest have been able not to suffer. Learn thou to suffer, and thou shalt be able not to suffer. What thou knowest not, I myself will teach thee. Thy God am I, not the God of the traitor. I would keep tune with holy souls. In me know thou the word of wisdom. Again with me say thou: Glory be to thee, Father; glory to thee, Word; glory to thee, Holy Ghost. And if thou wouldst know concerning me, what I was, know that with a word did I deceive all things and I was no whit deceived. I have leaped: but do thou understand the whole, and having understood it, say: Glory be to thee, Father. Amen.

97 Thus, my beloved, having danced with us the Lord went forth. And we as men gone astray or dazed with sleep fled this way and that. I, then, when I saw him suffer, did not even abide by his suffering, but fled unto the Mount of Olives, weeping at that which had befallen. And when he was crucified on the Friday, at the sixth hour of the day, darkness came upon all the earth. And my Lord standing in the midst of the cave and enlightening it, said: John, unto the multitude below in Jerusalem I am being crucified and pierced with lances and reeds, and gall and vinegar is given me to drink. But unto thee I speak, and what I speak hear thou. I put it into thy mind to come up into this mountain, that thou mightest hear those things which it behoveth a disciple to learn from his teacher and a man from his God.

98 And having thus spoken, he showed me a cross of light fixed (set up), and about the cross a great multitude, not having one form: and in it (the cross) was one form and one likenesst [so the MS.; I would read: and therein was one form and one likeness: and in the cross another multitude, not having one form]. And the Lord himself I beheld above the cross, not having any shape, but only a voice: and a voice not such as was familiar to us, but one sweet and kind and truly of God, saying unto me: John, it is needful that one should hear these things from me, for I have need of one that will hear. This cross of light is sometimes called the (or a) word by me for your sakes, sometimes mind, sometimes Jesus, sometimes Christ, sometimes door, sometimes a way, sometimes bread, sometimes seed, sometimes resurrection, sometimes Son, sometimes Father, sometimes Spirit, sometimes life, sometimes truth, sometimes faith, sometimes grace. And by these names it is called as toward men: but that which it is in truth, as conceived of in itself and as spoken of unto you (MS. us), it is the marking-off of all things, and the firm uplifting of things fixed out of things unstable, and the harmony of wisdom, and indeed wisdom in harmony [this last clause in the MS. is joined to the next: 'and being wisdom in harmony']. There are [places] of the right hand

and the left, powers also, authorities, lordships and demons, workings, threatenings, wraths, devils, Satan, and the lower root whence the nature of the things that come into being proceeded.

99 This cross, then, is that which fixed all things apart (al. joined all things unto itself) by the (or a) word, and separate off the things that are from those that are below (lit. the things from birth and below it), and then also, being one, streamed forth into all things (or, made all flow forth. I suggested: compacted all into [one]). But this is not the cross of wood which thou wilt see when thou goest down hence: neither am I he that is on the cross, whom now thou seest not, but only hearest his (or a) voice. I was reckoned to be that which I am not, not being what I was unto many others: but they will call me (say of me) something else which is vile and not worthy of me. As, then, the place of rest is neither seen nor spoken of, much more shall I, the Lord thereof, be neither seen [nor of spoken].

100 Now the multitude of one aspect (al. [not] of one aspect) that is about the cross is the lower nature: and they whom thou seest in the cross, if they have not one form, it is because not yet hath every member of him that came down been comprehended. But when the human nature (or the upper nature) is taken up, and the race which draweth near unto me and obeyeth my voice, he that now heareth me shall be united therewith, and shall no more be that which now he is, but above them, as I also now am. For so long as thou callest not thyself mine, I am not that which I am (or was): but if thou hear me, thou, hearing, shalt be as I am, and I shall be that which I was, when I [have]thee as I am with myself. For from me thou art that (which I am). Care not therefore for the many, and them that are outside the mystery despise; for know thou that I am wholly with the Father, and the Father with me.

101 Nothing, therefore, of the things which they will say of me have I suffered: nay, that suffering also which I showed unto thee and the rest in the dance, I will that it be called a mystery. For what thou art, thou seest, for I showed it thee; but what I am I alone know, and

no man else. Suffer me then to keep that which is mine, and that which is thine behold thou through me, and behold me in truth, that I am, not what I said, but what thou art able to know, because thou art akin thereto. Thou hearest that I suffered, yet did I not suffer; that I suffered not, yet did I suffer; that I was pierced, yet I was not smitten; hanged, and I was not hanged; that blood flowed from me, and it flowed not; and, in a word, what they say of me, that befell me not, but what they say not, that did I suffer. Now what those things are I signify unto thee, for I know that thou wilt understand. Perceive thou therefore in me the praising (al. slaying al. rest) of the (or a) Word (Logos), the piercing of the Word, the blood of the Word, the wound of the Word, the hanging up of the Word, the suffering of the Word, the nailing (fixing) of the Word, the death of the Word. And so speak I, separating off the manhood. Perceive thou therefore in the first place of the Word; then shalt thou perceive the Lord, and in the third place the man, and what he hath suffered.

102 When he had spoken unto me these things, and others which I know not how to say as he would have me, he was taken up, no one of the multitudes having beheld him. And when I went down I laughed them all to scorn, inasmuch as he had told me the things which they have said concerning him; holding fast this one thing in myself, that the Lord contrived all things symbolically and by a dispensation toward men, for their conversion and salvation.

103 Having therefore beheld, brethren, the grace of the Lord and his kindly affection toward us, let us worship him as those unto whom he hath shown mercy, not with our fingers, nor our mouth, nor our tongue, nor with any part whatsoever of our body, but with the disposition of our soul -even him who became a man apart from this body: and let us watch because (or we shall find that) now also he keepeth ward over prisons for our sake, and over tombs, in bonds and dungeons, in reproaches and insults, by sea and on dry land, in scourgings, condemnations, conspiracies, frauds, punishments, and in a word, he is with all of us, and himself suffereth with us when we

suffer, brethren. When he is called upon by each one of us, he endureth not to shut his ears to us, but as being everywhere he hearkeneth to all of us; and now both to me and to Drusiana, -forasmuch as he is the God of them that are shut upbringing us help by his own compassion.

104 Be ye also persuaded, therefore, beloved, that it is not a man whom I preach unto you to worship, but God unchangeable, God invincible, God higher than all authority and all power, and elder and mightier than all angels and creatures that are named, and all aeons. If then ye abide in him, and are builded up in him, ye shall possess your soul indestructible.

105 And when he had delivered these things unto the brethren, John departed, with Andronicus, to walk. And Drusiana also followed afar off with all the brethren, that they might behold the acts that were done by him, and hear his speech at all times in the Lord.

The remaining episode which is extant in the Greek is the conclusion of the book, the Death or Assumption of John. Before it must be placed the stories which we have only in the Latin (of 'Abdias' and another text by 'Mellitus', i.e. Melito), and the two or three isolated fragments.

(Lat. XIV.) Now on the next (or another) day Craton, a philosopher, had proclaimed in the market-place that he would give an example of the contempt of riches: and the spectacle was after this manner. He had persuaded two young men, the richest of the city, who were brothers, to spend their whole inheritance and buy each of them a jewel, and these they brake in pieces publicly in the sight of the people. And while they were doing this, it happened by chance that the apostle passed by. And calling Craton the philosopher to him, he said: That is a foolish despising of the world which is praised by the mouths of men, but long ago condemned by the judgement of God. For as that is a vain medicine whereby the disease is not extirpated, so is it a vain teaching by which the faults of souls and of conduct are not cured. But indeed my master taught a youth who desired to attain to eternal life, in these words; saying that if he would be perfect, he should sell all his goods and give to the poor, and so doing he would gain treasure in heaven and find the life that has no ending. And Craton said to him: Here the fruit of covetousness is set forth in the midst of men, and hath been broken to pieces. But if God is indeed thy master and willeth this to be, that the sum of the price of these jewels should be given to the poor, cause thou the gems to be restored whole, that what I have done for the praise of men, thou mayest do for the glory of him whom thou callest thy master. Then the blessed John gathered together the fragments of the gems, and holding them in his hands, lifted up his eyes to heaven and said: Lord Jesu Christ, unto whom nothing is impossible: who when the world was broken by the tree of concupiscence, didst restore it again in thy faithfulness by the tree of the cross: who didst give to one born blind the eyes which nature had denied him, who didst recall Lazarus, dead and buried, after the fourth day unto the light; and has subjected all diseases and all sicknesses unto the word of thy power: so also now do with these precious stones which these, not knowing the fruits of almsgiving, have broken in pieces for the praise of men: recover thou them, Lord, now by the hands of thine angels, that by their value the work of mercy may be fulfilled, and make these men believe in thee the unbegotten Father through thine only-begotten Son Jesus Christ our Lord, with the Holy Ghost the illuminator and sanctifier of the whole Church, world without end. And when the faithful who were with the apostle had answered and said Amen, the fragments of the gems were forthwith so joined in one that no mark at all that they had been broken remained in them. And Craton the philosopher, with his disciples, seeing this, fell at the feet of the apostle and believed thenceforth (or immediately) and was baptized, with them all, and began himself publicly to preach the faith of our Lord Jesus Christ.

XV. Those two brothers, therefore, of whom we spake, sold the gems which they had bought by the sale of their inheritance and gave the price to the poor; and thereafter a very great multitude of believers began to be joined to the apostle.

And when all this was done, it happened that after the same example, two honourable men of the city of the Ephesian sold all their goods and distributed them to the needy, and followed the apostle as he went through the cities preaching the word of God. But it came to pass, when they entered the city of Pergamum, that they saw their servants walking abroad arrayed in silken raiment and shining with the glory of this world: whence it happened that they were pierced with the arrow of the devil and became sad, seeing themselves poor and clad with a single cloak while their own servants were powerful and prosperous. But the apostle of Christ, perceiving these wiles of the devil, said: I see that ye have changed your minds and your countenances on this account, that, obeying the teaching of my Lord Jesus Christ, ye have given all ye had to the poor. Now, if ye desire to recover that which ye formerly possessed of gold, silver, and precious stones, bring me some straight rods, each of you a bundle. And when they had done so, he called upon the name of the Lord Jesus Christ, and they were turned into gold. And the apostle said to them: Bring me small stones from the seashore. And when they had done this also, he called upon the majesty of the Lord, and all the pebbles were turned into gems. Then the blessed John turned to those men and said to them: Go about to the goldsmiths and jewellers for seven days, and when ye have proved that these are true gold and true jewels, tell me. And they went, both of them, and after seven days returned to the apostle, saying: Lord, we have gone about the shops of all the goldsmiths, and they have all said that they never saw such pure gold. Likewise the jewellers have said the same, that they never saw such excellent and precious gems.

XVI. Then the holy John said unto them: Go, and redeem to you the lands which ye have sold, for ye have lost the estates of heaven. Buy yourselves silken raiment, that for a time ye may shine like the rose which showeth its fragrance and redness and suddenly fadeth away. For ye sighed at beholding your servants and groaned that ye were become poor. Flourish, therefore, that ye may fade: be rich for the time, that ye may be beggars for ever. Is not the Lord's hand able to make riches overflowing and unsurpassably glorious? but he hath appointed a conflict for souls, that they may believe that they shall have eternal riches, who for his name's sake have refused temporal wealth. Indeed, our master told us concerning a certain rich man who feasted every day and shone with gold and purple, at whose door lay a beggar, Lazarus, who desired to receive even the crumbs that fell from his table, and no man gave unto him. And it came to pass that on one day they died, both of them, and that beggar was taken into the rest which is in Abraham's bosom, but the rich man was cast into flaming fire: out of which he lifted up his eyes and saw Lazarus, and prayed him to dip his finger in water and cool his mouth for he was tormented in the flames. And Abraham answered him and said: Remember, son, that thou receivedst good things in thy life, but this Lazarus likewise evil things. Wherefore rightly is he now comforted while thou art tormented, and besides all this, a great gulf is fixed between you and us, so that neither can they come thence hither, nor hither thence. But he answered: I have five brethren: I pray that some one may go to warn them, that they come not into this flame. And Abraham said to him: They have Moses and the prophets, let them hear them. To that he answered: Lord, unless one rise up again, they will not believe. Abraham said to him: If they believe not Moses and the prophets, neither will they believe, if one rise again. And these words our Lord and Master confirmed by examples of mighty works: for when they said to him: Who hath come hither from thence, that we may believe him? he answered: Bring hither the dead whom ye have. And when they had brought unto him a young man which was dead (Ps.-Mellitus: three dead corpses), he was waked up by him as one that sleepeth, and confirmed all his words.

But wherefore should I speak of my Lord, when at this present there are those whom in his name and in your presence and sight I have raised from the dead: in whose name ye have seen palsied men healed, lepers cleansed, blind men enlightened, and many delivered from evil spirits ? But the riches of these mighty works they cannot have who have desired to have earthly wealth. Finally, when ye yourselves went unto the sick and called upon the name of Jesus Christ, they were healed: ye did drive out devils and restore light to the blind. Behold, this grace is taken from you, and ye are become wretched, who were mighty and great. And where as there was such fear of you upon the devils that at your bidding they left the men whom they possessed, now ye will be in fear of the devils. For he that loveth money is the servant of Mammon: and Mammon is the name of a devil who is set over carnal gains, and is the master of them that love the world. But even the lovers of the world do not possess riches, but are possessed of them. For it is out of reason that for one belly there should be laid up so much food as would suffice a thousand, and for one body so many garments as would furnish clothing for a thousand men. In vain, therefore, is that stored up which cometh not into use, and for whom it is kept, no man knoweth, as the Holy Ghost saith by the prophet: In vain is every man troubled who heapeth up riches and knoweth not for whom he gathereth them. Naked did our birth from women bring us into this light, destitute of food and drink: naked will the earth receive us which brought us forth. We possess in common the riches of the heaven, the brightness of the sun is equal for the rich and the poor, and likewise the light of the moon and the stars, the softness of the air and the drops of rain, and the gate of the church and the fount of sanctification and the forgiveness of sins, and the sharing in the altar, and the eating of the body and drinking of the blood of Christ, and the anointing of the chrism, and the grace of the giver, and the visitation of the Lord, and the pardon of sin: in all these the dispensing of the Creator is equal, without respect of persons. Neither doth the rich man use these gifts after one manner and the poor after another.

But wretched and unhappy is the man who would have something more than sufficeth him: for of this come heats of fevers rigours of cold, divers pains in all the members of the body, and he can neither be fed with food nor sated with drink, that covetousness may learn that money will not profit it, which being laid up bringeth to the keepers thereof anxiety by day and night, and suffereth them not even for an hour to be quiet and secure. For while they guard their houses against thieves, till their estate, ply the plough, pay taxes, build storehouses, strive for gain, try to baffle the attacks of the strong, and to strip the weak, exercise their wrath on whom they can, and hardly bear it from others, shrink not from playing at tables and from public shows, fear not to defile or to be defiled, suddenly do they depart out of this world, naked, bearing only their own sins with them, for which they shall suffer eternal punishment.

XVII. While the apostle was thus speaking, behold there was brought to him by his mother, who was a widow, a young man who thirty days before had first married a vvife. And the people which were waiting upon the burial came with the widowed mother and cast themselves at the apostle's feet all together with groans, weeping, and mourning, and besought him that in the name of his God, as he had done with Drusiana, so he would raise up this young man also. And there was so great weeping of them all that the apostle himself could hardly refrain from crying and tears. He cast himself down, therefore, in prayer, and wept a long time: and rising from prayer spread out his hands to heaven, and for a long space prayed within himself. And when he had so done thrice, he commanded the body which was swathed to be loosed, and said: Thou youth Stacteus, who for love of thy flesh hast quickly lost thy soul: thou youth which knewest not thy creator nor perceivedst the Saviour of men, and wast ignorant of thy true friend, and therefore didst fall into the snare of the worst enemy: behold, I have poured out tears and prayers unto my Lord for thine ignorance, that thou mayest rise from the dead, the bands of death being loosed, and declare unto these two, to Atticus and Eugenius, how great glory they have lost, and how great punishment they have incurred. Then Stacteus arose and worshipped the apostle, and began to reproach his disciples, saying: I beheld your angels vveeping, and the angels of Satan rejoicing at your overthrow. For now in a little time ye have lost the kingdom that was prepared for you, and the dwellingplaces builded of shining stones, full of joy, of feasting and delights, full of everlasting life and eternal light: and have gotten yourselves places of darkness, full of dragons, of roaring flames, of torments, and punishments unsurpassable, of pains and anguish, fear and horrible trembling. Ye have lost the places full of unfading flowers, shining, full of the sounds of instruments of music (organs), and have gotten on the other hand places wherein roaring and howling and mourning ceaseth not day nor night. Nothing else remaineth for you save to ask the apostle of the Lord that like as he hath raised me to life, he would raise you also from death unto salvation and bring back your souls which now are blotted out of the book of life.

XVIII. Then both he that had been raised and all the people together with Atticus and Eugenius, cast themselves at the apostle's feet and besought him to intercede for them with the Lord. Unto whom the holy apostle gave this answer: that for thirty days they should offer penitence to God, and in that space pray especially that the rods of gold might return to their nature and likewise the stones return to the meanness wherein they were made. And it came to pass that after thirty days were accomplished, and neither the rods were turncd into wood nor the gems into pebbles, Atticus and Eugenius came and said to the apostle: Thou hast always taught mercy, and preached forgiveness, and bidden that one man should spare another. And if God willeth that a man should forgive a man, how much more shall he, as he is God, both forgive and spare men. We are confounded for our sin: and whereas we have cried with our eyes which lusted after the world, we do now repent with eyes that weep. We pray thee, Lord, we pray thee, apostle of God, show in deed that mercy which in word thou hast always promised. Then the holy John said unto them as they wept and repented, and all interceded for them likewise: Our Lord God used these words when he spake concerning sinners: I will not the death of a sinner, but I will rather that he be converted and live. For when the Lord Jesus Christ taught us concerning the penitent, he said: Verily I say unto you, there is great joy in heaven over one sinner that repenteth and turneth himself from his sins: and there is more joy over him than over ninety and nine which have not sinned. Wherefore I would have you know that the Lord accepteth the repentance of these men. And he turned unto Atticus and Eugenius and said: Go, carry back the rods unto the wood whence ye took them, for now are they returned to their own nature, and the stones unto the sea-shore, for they are become common stones as they were before. And when this was accomplished, they received again the grace which they had lost, so that again they cast out devils as before time and healed the sick and enlightened the blind, and daily the Lord did many mighty works by their means.

XIX tells shortly the destruction oi the temple of Ephesus and the conversion of 12,000 people.

Then follows the episode of the poison-cup in a form which probably represents the story in the Leucian Acts. (We have seen that the late Greek texts place it at the beginning, in the presence of Domitian.)

XX. Now when Aristodemus, who was chief priest of all those idols, saw this, filled with a wicked spirit, he stirred up sedition among the people, so that one people prepared themselves to fight against the other. And John turned to him and said: Tell me, Aristodemus, what can I do to take away the anger from thy soul? And Aristodemus said: If thou wilt have me believe in thy God, I will give thee poison to drink, and if thou drink it, and die not, it will appear that thy God is true. The apostle answered: If thou give me poison to drink, when I call on the name of my Lord, it will not be able to harm me. Aristodemus said again: I will that thou first see others drink it and die straightway that so thy heart may recoil from that cup. And the blessed John said: I have told thee already that I am prepared to drink it that thou mayest believe on the Lord Jesus Christ when thou seest me whole after the cup of poison. Aristodemus therefore went to the proconsul and asked of him two men who were to undergo the sentence of death. And when he had set them in the midst of the market-place before all the people, in the sight of the apostle he made them drink the poison: and as soon as they had drunk it, they gave up the ghost. Then Aristodemus turned to John and said: Hearken to me and depart from thy teaching wherewith thou callest away the people from the worship of the gods; or take and drink this, that thou mayest show that thy God is almighty, if after thou hast drunk, thou canst remain whole. Then the blessed Jolm, as they lay dead which had drunk the poison, like a fearless and brave man took the cup, and making the sign of the cross, spake thus: My God, and the Father of our Lord Jesus Christ, by whose word the heavens were established, unto whom all things are subject, whom all creation serveth, whom all power obeyeth, feareth, and trembleth, when we call on thee for succour: whose name the serpent hearing is still, the dragon fleeth, the viper is quiet, the toad (which is called a frog) is still and strengthless, the scorpion is quenched, the basilisk vanquished, and the phalangia (spider) doth no hurt -in a word, all venomous things, and the fiercest reptiles and noisome beasts, are pierced (or covered with darkness). [Ps.- Mellitus adds: and all roots hurtful to the health of men dry up.] Do thou, I say, quench the venom of this poison, put out the deadly workings thereof, and void it of the strength which it hath in it: and grant in thy sight unto all these whom thou hast created, eyes that they may see, and ears that they may hear and a heart that they may understand thy greatness. And when he had thus said, he armed his mouth and all his body with the sign of the cross and drank all that was in the cup. And after be had drunk, he said: I ask that they for whose sake I have drunk, be turned unto thee, O Lord, and by thine enlightening receive the salvation which is in thee.

And when for the space of three hours the people saw that John was of a cheerful countenance, and that there was no sign at all of paleness or fear in him, they began to cry out with a loud voice: He is the one true God whom John worshippeth.

XXI. But Aristodemus even so believed not, though the people reproached him: but turned unto John and said: This one thing I lack -if thou in the name of thy God raise up these that have died by this poison, my mind will be cleansed of all doubt. When he said that, the people rose against Aristodemus saying: We will burn thee and thine house if thou goest on to trouble the apostle further with thy words. John, therefore, seeing that there was a fierce sedition, asked for silence, and said in the hearing of all: The first of the virtues of God which we ought to imitate is patience, by which we are able to bear with the foolishness of unbelievers. Wherefore if Aristodemus is still held by unbelicf, let us loose the knots of his unbelief. He shall be compelled, even though late, to acknowledge his creator -for I will not cease from this work until a remedy shall bring help to his wounds, and like physicians which have in their hands a sick man needing medicine, so also, if Aristodemus be not yet cured by that which hath now been done, he shall be cured by that which I will now do. And he called Aristodemus to him, and gave him his coat, and he himself stood clad only in his mantle. And Aristodemus said to him: Wherefore hast thou given me thy coat? John said to him: That thou mayest even so be put to shame and depart from thine unbelief. And Aristodemus said: And how shall thy coat make me to depart from unbelief? The apostle answered: Go and cast it upon the bodies of the dead, and thou shalt say thus: The apostle of our Lord Jesus Christ hath sent me that in his name ye may rise again, that all may know that life and death are servants of my Lord Jesus Christ. Which when Aristodemus had done, and had seen them rise, he worshipped John, and ran quickly to the proconsul and began to say with a loud voice: Hear me, hear me, thou proconsul; I think thou rememberest that I have often stirred up thy wrath against John and devised many things against him daily, wherefore I fear lest I feel his wrath: for he is a god hidden in the form of a man and hath drunk poison, and not only continueth whole, but them also which had died by the poison he hath recalled to life by my means, by the touch of his coat, and they have no mark of death upon them. Which when the proconsul heard he said: And what wilt thou have me to do? Aristodemus answered: Let us go and fall at his feet and ask pardon, and whatever he commandeth us let us do. Then they came together and cast themselves down and besought forgiveness: and he received them and offered prayer and thanksgiving to God, and he ordained them a fast of a week, and when it was fulfilled he baptized them in the name of the Lord Jesus Christ and his Almighty Father and the Holy Ghost the illuminator. [And when thev were baptized, with all their house and their servants and their kindred, they brake all their idols and built a church in the name of Saint John: wherein he himself was taken up, in manner following :]

This bracketed sentence, of late complexion, serves to introduce the last episode of the book.

[M.R. James gives two additional fragments that do not fit in any other place. These fragments are very broken and are not of much use for this present project. However, if there is interest in them, they can be found on pages 264-6 of the text.]

The last episode of these Acts (as is the case with several others of the Apocryphal Acts) was preservcd separately for reading in church on the Saint's day. We have it in at least nine Greck manuscripts, and in many versions: Latin, Syriac, Armenian, Coptic, Ethiopic, Slavonic.

106 John therefore continued with the brethren, rejoicing in the Lord. And on the morrow, being the Lord's day, and all the brethren being gathered together, he began to say unto them: Brethren and fellow-servants and coheirs and partakers with me in the kingdom of the Lord, ye know the Lord, hovv many mighty works he hath granted you by my means, how many wonders, healings, signs, how great spiritual gifts, teachings, governings, refreshings, ministries,

knowledges, glories, graces, gifts, beliefs, communions, all which ye have seen given you by him in your sight, yet not seen by these eyes nor heard by these ears. Be ye therefore stablished in him, remembering him in your every deed, knowing the mystery of the dispensation which hath come to pass towards men, for what cause the Lord hath l accomplished it. He beseecheth you by me, brethren, and entreateth you, desiring to remain without grief, without insult, not conspired against, not chastened: for he knoweth even the insult that cometh of you, he knoweth even dishonour, he knoweth even conspiracy, he knoweth even chastisement, from them that hearken not to his commandments.

107 Let not then our good God be grieved, the compassionate, the merciful, the holy, the pure, the undefiled, the immaterial, the only, the one, the unchangeable, the simple, the guileless, the unwrathful, even our God Jesus Christ, who is above every name that we can utter or conceive, and more exalted. Let him rejoice with us because we walk aright, let him be glad because we live purely, let him be refreshed because our conversation is sober. Let him be without care because we live continently, let him be pleased because we communicate one with another, let him smile because we are chaste, let him be merry because we love him. These things I now speak unto you, brethren, because I am hasting unto the work set before me, and already being perfected by the Lord. For what else could I have to say unto you? Ye have the pledge of our God, ye have the earnest of his goodness, ye have his presence that cannot be shunned. If, then, ye sin no more, he forgiveth you that ye did in ignorance: but if after that ye have known him and he hath had mercy on you, ye walk again in the like deeds, both the former will be laid to your charge, and also ye will not have a part nor mercy before him.

108 And when he had spoken this unto them, he prayed thus: O Jesu who hast woven this crown with thy weaving, who hast joined together these many blossoms into the unfading flower of thy cormtenance, who hast sown in them these words: thou only tender

of thy servants, and physician who healest freely: only doer of good and despiser of none, only merciful and lover of men, only saviour and righteous, only seer of all, who art in all and everywhere present and containing all things and filling all things: Christ Jesu, God, Lord, that with thy gifts and thy mercy shelterest them that trust in thee, that knowest clearly the wiles and the assaults of him that is everywhere our adversary, which he deviseth against us: do thou only, O Lord, succour thy servants by thy visitation. Even so, Lord.

109 And he asked for bread, and gave thanks thus: What praise or what offering or what thanksgiving shall we, breaking this bread, name save thee only, O Lord Jesu? We glorify thy name that was said by the Father: we glorify thy name that was said through the Son (or we glorify the name of Father that was said by thee . . . the name of Son that was said by thee): we glorify thine entering of the Door. We glorify the resurrection shown unto us by thee. We glorify thy way, we glorify of thee the seed, the word, the grace, the faith, the salt, the unspeakable (al. chosen) pearl, the treasure, the plough, the net, the greatness, the diadem, him that for us was called Son of man, that gave unto us truth, rest, knowledge, power, the commandment, the confidence, hope, love, liberty, refuge in thee. For thou, Lord, art alone the root of immortality, and the fount of incorruption, and the seat of the ages: called by all these names for us now that calling on thee by them we may make known thy greatness which at the present is invisible unto us, but visible only unto the pure, being portrayed in thy manhood only.

110 And he brake the bread and gave unto all of us, praying over each of the brethren that he might be worthy of the grace of the Lord and of the most holy eucharist. And he partook also himself likewise, and said: Unto me also be there a part with you, and: Peace be with you, my beloved.

111 After that he said unto Verus: Take with thee some two men, with baskets and shovels, and follow me. And Verus without delay did as he was bidden by John the servant of God. The blessed John

therefore went out of the house and walked forth of the gates, having told the more part to depart from him. And when he was come to the tomb of a certain brother of ours he said to the young men: Dig, my children. And they dug and he was instant with them yet more, saying: Let the trench be deeper. And as they dug he spoke unto them the word of God and exhorted them that were come with him out of the house, edifying and perfecting them unto the greatness of God, and praying over each one of us. And when the young men had finished the trench as he desired, we knowing nothing of it, he took off his garments wherein he was clad and laid them as it were for a pallet in the bottom of the trench: and standing in his shift only he stretched his hands upward and prayed thus:

112 O thou that didst choose us out for the apostleship of the Gentiles: O God that sentest us into the world: that didst reveal thyself by the law and the prophets: that didst never rest, but alway from the foundation of the world savedst them that were able to be saved: that madest thyself known through all nature: that proclaimedst thyself even among beasts: that didst make the desolate and savage soul tame and quiet: that gavest thyself to it when it was athirst for thy words: that didst appear to it in haste when it was dying: that didst show thyself to it as a law when it was sinking into lawlessness: that didst manifest thyself to it when it had been vanquished by Satan: that didst overcome its adversary when it fled unto thee: that avest it thine hand and didst raise it up from the things of Hades: that didst not leave it to walk after a bodily sort (in the body): that didst show to it its own enemy: that hast made for it a clear knowledge toward thee: O God, Jesu, the Father of them that are above the heavens, the Lord of them that are in the heavens, the law of them that are in the other, the course of them that are in the air, the keeper of them that are on the earth, the fear of them that are under the earth, the grace of them that are thine own: receive also the soul of thy John, which it may be is accounted worthy by thee.

113 O thou who hast kept me until this hour for thyself and

untouched by union with a woman: who when in my youth I desired to marry didst appear unto me and say to me: John I have need of thee: who didst prepare for me also a sickness of the body: who when for the third time I would marry didst forthwith prevent me, and then at the third hour of the day saidst unto me on the sea: John, if thou hadst not been mine, I would have suffered thee to marry: who for two years didst blind me (or afflict mine eyes), and grant me to mourn and entreat thee: who in the third year didst open the eyes of my mind and also grant me my visible eyes: who when I saw clearly didst ordain that it should be grievous to me to look upon a woman: who didst save me from the temporal fantasy and lead me unto that which endureth always: who didst rid me of the foul madness that is in the flesh: who didst take me from the bitter death and establish me on thee alone: who didst muzzle the secret disease of my soul and cut off the open deed: who didst afflict and banish him that raised tumult in me: who didst make my love of thee spotless: who didst make my joining unto thee perfect and unbroken: who didst give me undoubting faith in thee, who didst order and make clear my inclination toward thee: thou who givest unto every man the due reward of his works, who didst put into my soul that I should have no possession save thee only: for what is more precious than thee? Now therefore Lord, whereas I have accomplished the dispensation wherewith I was entrusted, account thou me worthy of thy rest, and grant me that end in thee which is salvation unspeakable and unutterable.

114 And as I come unto thee, let the fire go backward, let the darkness be overcome, let the gulf be without strength, let the furnace die out, let Gehenna be quenched. Let angels follow, let devils fear, let rulers be broken, Iet powers fall; let the places of the right hand stand fast, let them of the left hand not remain. Let the devil be muzzled, let Satan be derided, let his wrath be burned out, Iet his madness be stilled, let his vengeance be ashamed, let his assault be in pain, let his children be smitten and all his roots plucked up. And

grant me to accomplish the journey unto thee without suffering insolence or provocation, and to receive that which thou hast promised unto them that live purely and have loved thee only.

115 And having sealed himself in every part, he stood and said: Thou art with me, O Lord Jesu Christ: and laid himself down in the trench where he had strown his garments: and having said unto us: Peace be with you, brethren, he gave up his spirit rejoicing.

The less good Greek manuscripts and some versions are not content with this simple ending. The Latin says that after the prayer a great light appeared over the apostle for the space of an hour, so bright that no one could look at it.

Then he laid himself down and gave up the ghost.) We who were there rejoiced, some of us, and some mourned. . . . And forthwith manna issuing from the tomb was seen of all, which manna that place produceth even unto this day, &c.

But perhaps the best conclusion is that of one Greek manuscript:

We brought a linen cloth and spread it upon him, and went into the city. And on the day following we went forth and found not his body, for it was translated by the power of our Lord Jesus Christ, unto whom be glory, &c.

Another says:

On the morrow we dug in the place, and him we found not, but only his sandals, and the earth moving (lit. springing up like a well), and after that we remembered that which was spoken by the Lord unto Peter, &c.

Augustine (on John xxi) reports the belief that in his time the earth over the grave was seen to move as if stirred by John's breathing.

www.ingramcontent.com/pod-product-compliance
Lightning Source LLC
Chambersburg PA
CBHW051849040426
42447CB00006B/772